FAMOUS
HOCKEY PLAYERS

FAMOUS
HOCKEY PLAYERS

by Trent Frayne

ILLUSTRATED WITH PHOTOGRAPHS

Dodd, Mead & Company · New York

TO JUNE

ISBN: 0-396-06848-0
Library of Congress Catalog Card Number: 73-7095
Printed in the United States of America
by Vail-Ballou Press, Inc., Binghamton, N. Y.

CONTENTS

HOWIE MORENZ

[1902-1937]

O_N THE WINDY, wintery night of March 8, 1937, Howie Morenz died on the floor of a hospital room in Montreal. He was thirty-four years old and he died of a broken heart.

Howie Morenz was more than merely one of the greatest hockey players who ever lived. He became a part of the national folklore, a symbol of a hockey era that is now only a memory, of a time when the ice heroes were a roughhewn and usually hard-drinking bunch, fiercely loyal to their teams. Even the smoke-filled rinks in which they played had a warmer look and smell than the antiseptic palaces that came along in the years of the National Hockey League's expansion in the late 1960s. To the millworkers, tram drivers, and off-duty cabbies who jammed one end of the Forum in Montreal and called themselves, with magnificent irony, the Millionaires, Morenz was a superhuman figure. Between periods they toasted him boisterously in bathtub gin. Their battle cry, *"Les Canadiens sont là"* never reached such frenzy as when Morenz started winding up behind his own net with an odd little bouncing jig that sent him hurtling down the ice in an exhilarating moment of excitement and reached its crescendo when he threw himself between the defensemen and whistled the puck past the goaltender.

For the twelve years that he wore the uniform of the Canadiens Morenz was an idol. In the years following that bleak March night in 1937 when he died he became a legend.

Although Morenz was of German origin, his volatile fans embraced the inspired fiction that he was a Swiss with a French spirit. His name was no more strange to their tongues than the names of his teammates—Mantha, Mondou, Lepine, Joliat, and Battleship Leduc. He was far more than a Canadien hero. To youngsters all across Canada he was to hockey what Babe Ruth was to baseball and Jack Dempsey to boxing—a larger-than-life figure who could do things no one else could do, against greater odds. When Morenz duped a defenseman it was David slaying Goliath.

Once Morenz received a terrible body check from Red Horner of Toronto, the league's bad man who weighed 220 and was six-feet-two. The check knocked Morenz thirty feet across the ice into a corner where he lay still for a moment. Then he climbed to his feet, skated shakily toward his own end of the rink, and retrieved the puck. He bounced into stride, catapulted directly toward Horner, faked a swerve to deceive the defenseman, and leaped nimbly past him and scored, mere seconds after Horner had flattened him.

When the Canadiens were hard-pressed it was Morenz who brought a hoarse roar from the Millionaires and happy nods from the millions who followed his exploits on radio and in the newspapers. And Morenz never had such modern advantages as the forward pass, the center red line, and the seemingly unending schedules in which to pile up his goals. In the 1929–30 season, for instance, he scored forty goals in forty-four games. In his fourteen years in the NHL, the schedule progressively increased from twenty-four to forty-

8

eight games. In two of his seasons he was desperately un-happy in the uniforms of the Chicago Black Hawks and the New York Rangers, and when the return to his beloved Ca-nadiens came in his final season a broken leg curtailed his joyous reunion. The crux of his career embraced the eight seasons from 1924–25 through 1931–32 when he played 334 games and scored 217 goals, a time period representing about four and a half seasons of post-expansion scheduling.

Morenz led the Canadiens to the Stanley Cup three times and he won the Hart Trophy three times as the league's most valuable player. He won the NHL scoring champion-ship twice and was listed in the top five scorers eight times. His value wasn't merely in the number of goals he scored; he had a way of getting pay-off goals, too. One night in 1930 the Black Hawks, with their superb goaltender Charlie Gardiner and a total commitment to defensive strategy, held the Cana-diens to a tie until ten minutes to two in the morning—the longest overtime game to that point in hockey history. Finally, Morenz performing indefatigably barged past big Taffy Abel to beat Gardiner with the goal that eliminated the Hawks from Cup playoffs.

And of course his speed was a defensive asset, too. Once in Ottawa defenseman Alex Smith got a breakaway and had a jump of maybe fifty feet on Morenz on the 200-foot ice sur-face. But Morenz caught him from behind, batted the puck into a corner, picked it up, passed Smith going the other way, and flipped the puck to Aurel Joliat for a goal before the Ottawa team could regain its composure.

The Morenz skating style was as spectacular as his speed. His flying arms and bouncing stride gave him a unique whirlwind flair, though it's a fact that legend tended to make him swifter on his skates than history records. Once, in a match race at the Forum, Hec Kilrea of Ottawa, a platinum blond who later became a great favorite in Detroit, circled the rink carrying the puck in slightly faster time than Morenz. The incredulous Millionaires dismissed the evidence of their traitorous eyes: *"Enfin,* Howie let him win as a kindness." Morenz's following of thousands of idolizing kids in Canada didn't try to explain it; they just didn't believe it.

But even opposing players, who took a little more realistic view of Morenz, were inclinded to believe there wasn't much he couldn't do. Charlie Conacher, who played for Toronto in the latter stages of Morenz's career, once recalled Howie telling him earnestly: "Chuck, give me one good defenseman and any goaltender in this league and I'll beat any team for twenty minutes." And Conacher added, "There were nights when I figured he could have; don't forget, this was a time when there was no red line at center."

Morenz was the most sought-after player in the game. After one thrilling New York demonstration in 1926 when hockey was just getting properly organized there, the Rangers offered $60,000 for him; he had scored three goals including the winner in overtime. The Stanley Cup champion Montreal Maroons, the Canadiens' English-language crosstown rivals, learned of the offer and bid $75,000. But Leo Dandurand, owner of the Canadiens, declined both offers which, in 1926, represented roughly a year's payroll for an NHL club. "Morenz," said the dapper little Dandurand, "is beyond price."

Morenz was called the Stratford Streak because he played in an era when sportswriters steadfastly refused to permit a star athlete to go through life without some sort of purple sobriquet ("The Sultan of Swat," "Little Miss Poker Face," "The Manassa Mauler," "The Big Train"). Morenz made his early impression in hockey in the little Western Ontario town of Stratford which later became renowned for its annual Shakespeare Festival. He had been born near there in a hamlet called Mitchell on September 21, 1902, the youngest in a family of six that included brothers Wilf and Ezra and sisters Erma, Freda, and Gertrude. Morenz's parents emigrated from Germany prior to World War I and settled amid a wide swatch of German immigrants around Stratford and Kitchener (a town whose name was changed from Berlin during the war).

Howie's mother had hoped he'd be musical and she burdened him with piano lessons; he usually skipped his practice sessions to play hockey on the Thames River with crude sticks and chunks of coal. He was a goaltender for a time, wearing leg pads improvised of magazines stuffed into his stockings. In his first organized game in the Mitchell rink he gave up twenty-one goals and instantly became a forward. A few years later, after he'd established himself as a goal-scorer, the memory of his debut still rankled. One night against Toronto Balmy Beach he asked the coach to let him play in goal. The score was 3–3 late in the game. Goaltender Morenz stopped a shot and saw an opening. He sped down the ice in his heavy padding and scored the winning goal.

The family moved to Stratford when Morenz was fourteen, and he played for the juniors, the intermediates, and the Grand Trunk Railway's commercial-league team in his first year in the new town. In one period of eleven days he played twelve games for the three teams and traveled 2000 miles. One night in Montreal he scored eleven goals for the intermediates; the next night he scored six for the juniors in Kitchener. In spite of this unlikely record, though, he was not overly confident. Returning to Stratford once from Montreal he stopped in Toronto to watch the professional St. Pats, forerunners to the Maple Leafs, play an NHL game with the Ottawa Senators. "You don't have to worry about me becoming a professional," he told his mother when he arrived home. "Those fellows are far too good."

He played endlessly, hurt and well. He broke a toe one afternoon working in the railway machine shop, but that night he jumped off the bench to score the winning goal against Kitchener. When the game ended his toe was so swollen that his boot had to be cut from his foot. Another night a Stratford teammate, Frank Carson, slammed a car door on Howie's finger, almost severing it. A doctor set and splinted the finger and Morenz reached the rink an hour early so he could be dressed and have his glove covering his bandaged finger when the coach, Bill Gerby, arrived. Unaware of his star player's injury Gerby gave him full ice-time and Morenz scored four goals and assisted in four others.

If Morenz had no early confidence in his ability to play with the pros, it was a conviction not shared by them. Charlie Querrie, who ran the Toronto St. Pats, offered him a flat $1000 to play in the team's five remaining games of the 1922–23 season. Montreal's Leo Dandurand offered $2500 for the twenty-four game season of 1923–24 and grew concerned when Lou Marsh, a referee and sportswriter, telephoned him from Toronto that the St. Pats were hot after Morenz. Dandurand dispatched Canadien coach Cecil Hart to Stratford with a pocketful of folding money. When Hart offered to pay a $45 tailor's bill and give Morenz $300 to settle a number of other small debts, Howie agreed to play for the Canadiens. Stratford fans and team officials implored him to reconsider. Letters of protest were sent to Dandurand, and a minister wrote to a Toronto newspaper decrying the audacity of the Canadiens in "luring an underage boy (Howie was not quite twenty-one) to the wicked city of Montreal." Distressed by the furor, Morenz wrote Dandurand on August 10, 1923:

> I am enclosing check and contract to play Hockey with your club owing to Several reasons of which family and work are the most to consider I find it impossible to leave Stratford. I am sorry if I have caused you expense and inconvenience and trust you will accept the returned contract in a Sportsmanlike way.

Dandurand learned that Morenz was getting $800 a year as an amateur player and he threatened "to blow the lid off amateur hockey" if the Ontario Hockey Association didn't persuade Morenz to honor the contract. Howie made a trip to Montreal to plead personally with Dandurand. He spent an afternoon with the Dandurand family, had dinner with them, and was persuaded by the suave, debonaire Dandurand to join the Canadiens after all.

When Morenz went to training camp in the late autumn of 1923, Montreal's top forward line had Odie Cleghorn at center with Aurel Joliat at left wing and Billy Boucher at right wing. One morning when Cleghorn was nursing a bruised leg, Coach Cecil Hart sent young Morenz into Cleghorn's center position, and that was the end of Cleghorn. The Stratford Streak was soon the focus of training-camp news, carefully attended by the fine French hand of Leo Dandurand. With World War I only five years ended, Dandurand wasn't about to affront the volatile burghers of Montreal's predominantly French population by foisting a star of German extraction upon them; he publicized him as a Swiss, and although most of the fans were familiar with Morenz's skills from past exposure they were delighted to toast their new hero from "near Zurich." Particularly were they enthralled when Morenz's rink-length dashes and his wicked shot helped the Canadiens to victory over the haughty Senators from Ottawa in the NHL playoffs. The Canadiens then traveled to Vancouver in the Stanley Cup playdowns and won the series in two straight games by scores of 3–2 and 1–1. They played Calgary in the Stanley Cup final where goaltender Georges Vezina was superb in another straight-game conquest. Joliat, Boucher, and their young center Morenz skated circles around the Calgary defense and inspired victories by 6–1 and 3–0.

Boston and the Maroons joined the four-team NHL the following season, and Pittsburgh and the New York Americans came in a year after that. In 1926–27 the NHL completed its first great expansion, two divisions of five teams each, adding Detroit, Chicago, and the New York Rangers. Morenz led the Canadian Division in scoring through the next two seasons. He was a fierce competitor. Once, in a playoff game in Boston he faced off in overtime opposite Cooney Weiland of the Bruins. The puck flew in the air as their sticks clashed. Weiland took a half-swing and bounced the puck into the Canadien net for the winning goal. At four o'clock next morning Montreal sportswriter Elmer Ferguson answered a knock on his hotel-room door in Boston and found Morenz there. "He was in complete despair," Ferguson related years later. "He'd been walking the streets since the game ended, berating himself for Weiland's goal."

For all his competitiveness Morenz harbored no grudges. One night in Detroit Hec Kilrea piled into him and knocked him heavily to the ice. Morenz responded by up-ending Kilrea the next time the Detroit flash had the puck.

Kilrea leaped to his feet, brought his stick down on Morenz's head, and split open a long gash on his forehead. Kilrea faced suspension when he was paraded before league president Frank Calder. Morenz appeared at the hearing and told Calder he'd been as much to blame as Kilrea. "I don't think he meant it," he said with a small smile, fingering the adhesive tape across his scalp. Calder dismissed Kilrea with a warning.

Morenz's fearlessness on the ice belied his size. He was five-feet-eight and weighed only about 170. He looked heavier because, as Charlie Conacher once put it, "all his weight's in his face." He had a wide high forehead from which black hair lay smoothly back, wide-set brown eyes, the suggestion of jowls, and a perpetual five-o'clock shadow. Still, he loved the violent exchanges, the speed of the game, and the roar of the fiery partisans who were his Forum legion.

He was a companionable free-spender, an easy mark for people who wrote him hard-luck stories and for panhandlers. In summer he played golf nearly every day or worked in the pari-mutuel wickets at a Montreal race track. The day before he married Mary McKay of Montreal in 1926 he lost $1500 on the horses and cheerfully borrowed money from Dandurand on his next year's contract to pay for the honeymoon.

In this period, life was lush and filled with tomorrows. He had money in his pocket, hundreds of friends, and encountered adulation everywhere. One Saturday afternoon he sat in sportswriter Elmer Ferguson's home drinking beer and eating limburger cheese with onions. "When we ran out of onions Howie switched to garlic," Ferguson once recalled distastefully. "My wife couldn't stand the smell so she bought us some turkey legs and then left the house. I told Morenz he was full of beer and reeked of garlic. 'You'll never play hockey tonight,' I said. He laughed at me, and that night he scored three goals."

His great shot made him the scourge of goaltenders. "He could shoot harder than anybody I see around these days," Roy Worters remembered years later after the invention of the slapshot. Worters, who played goal for the Pittsburgh Pirates and the New York Americans for twelve NHL seasons, once called Morenz the fastest skater he'd ever seen. "When he'd wind up behind that net, he wasn't No. 7," Worters said. "He was No. 777—just a blur."

But, inevitably, there came the long nights when Morenz was no longer a blur to opposing goaltenders, when the great stride became a fraction shorter and the whizzing shot a shade less blistering. The transition did not come quickly and it wasn't always perceptible, but by the spring of 1933 Morenz had fallen to ninth place among the scorers and the Canadiens were lagging in the standings. One night Pit Lepine replaced Morenz at center on Montreal's top line. Morenz brooded over the demotion.

By spring 1934 Morenz hadn't regained his form, and his spirits hit a sickening low one night in the Forum when part of the Montreal crowd booed him. Cheers from the loyal Millionaires quickly drowned the boos but Leo Dandurand later recalled that Morenz went to him after that game "sobbing like a child." The idea of selling Morenz to another team had been unthinkable during Howie's magnificent years but now, apparently, it began to grow thinkable. Dandurand insisted in later years that the prospect of the volatile fans turning on a man who had meant so much to the Canadiens weighed heavily on his thinking. To save Morenz from that, Dandurand claimed, he decided to trade him. And he did, to Chicago, in the summer of 1934.

Morenz couldn't believe it. The Canadiens were his life, the Millionaires were as close to him as the players who'd been his teammates for eleven years. He walked the streets of Montreal trying to reconcile himself to the fact of Dandurand's decision. One night he returned home to his sleeping family. His wife found him sitting in the living room staring blankly at the dark floor. Tears were flowing down his cheeks.

Later Morenz reacted as he'd always reacted to a body blow—violently. He denounced Dandurand as an owner devoid of sentiment and loyalty, reacting impulsively to what Morenz claimed was nothing more than a bad year. He insisted he was far from through. Still, the record showed that he'd slipped from twenty-four goals to fourteen in the 1932–33 season, and down to eight goals during 1933–34.

In Chicago, things were scarcely better for him. The barnlike stadium with its callous fans was a different world from the familiar old Forum and the excitable Millionaires. Morenz didn't get along with Major Frederic McLaughlin, the rich and irascible Chicago owner, of whom he later said, "He's a tough man to work for, always waiting to jump on a player who has an off night." Morenz played well enough there. The Hawks were second in their division to Boston. The one-time Stratford Streak had only eight goals but he registered twenty-six assists and was third-highest point getter among Hawk players. But when he returned to Chicago for a second season, the snappish McLaughlin was soon hounding him. After the Canadiens beat the Hawks 2–1 one night, the owner stomped into the dressing room, stopped in front of Morenz, pointed an accusing finger at him, and said the Hawks would have had at least a tie had he played better. The once-fiery Morenz sat silent, his head bowed.

When he was benched for the next two games he went to McLaughlin and asked to be traded. "I'm not helping you sitting on the bench and I might be going stale," he told the owner. A few days later McLaughlin made a straight player trade with the Rangers, Morenz for a winger named Glenn Brydson. The trade seared Morenz's pride; three years earlier Brydson couldn't even have played on a line with him.

New York's tall and distinguished Lester Patrick, acknowledged as the league's best general manager and coach, tried Morenz at left wing beside Frank Boucher and Cecil Dillon. In a game in Toronto Morenz took a pass from Boucher, cut swiftly in on the Toronto goaltender George Hainsworth, and scored with a rising shot. He waved his stick jubilantly, overjoyed, and for a time his confidence was restored. But in eighteen games with the Rangers he scored only one other goal, and had four assists.

Then in the summer of 1936 Cecil Hart, Morenz's coach for ten years who had been replaced the year Morenz went to Chicago, returned to the Montreal bench, and one of his first moves was to buy Morenz's contract from the Rangers and reunite him with his longtime leftwing sidekick Aurel Joliat. Morenz was thirty-four when he went to training camp, and to the surprise of most hockey people he soon began to get back in stride. His deft passes to Joliat, and to his rightwinger, Johnny Gagnon, lifted that pair high in the scoring lists, and late in January the three of them were among the NHL's top ten scorers, Morenz with four goals and sixteen assists. Then on January 28 in a game against Chicago in the Forum, Morenz was bumped into the boards by Hawk defenseman Earl Seibert who caught the Canadien center off-balance. Morenz's left leg twisted under him as his skate caught in the boards and he broke three bones in the ankle and one in the leg.

And this, as it turned out, was the tragic climax to the hockey career of Howie Morenz. Slowly he accepted the terrible suspicion that he'd heard a crowd roar to his fiery play for the last time, and the knowledge turned him morose. He had lived high and spent his money as fast as he'd made it. He had provided little insurance for his family. His one major investment, a restaurant on St. Catherine Street in Montreal, had gone sour and had cost him a considerable sum.

Players from visiting teams and his Montreal friends streamed into St. Luke's Hospital to sit with Morenz, almost always bringing a bottle of Canadian rye to liven up proceedings, and Morenz kept pace with most of them. By day he chatted animatedly with his visitors. By night he took sedatives to relieve his physical pain and mental turmoil. He never admitted to his visitors that he knew his hockey career was ended, but close friends insisted that this knowledge, together with the original shock of having been traded away by the Canadiens, left scars that never mended.

When he had been lying in bed for a month, pale and drawn and fretful, his nerves gave way. But, as he'd always done, he battled back and still insisted to visitors that he'd be wearing No. 7 again next season, better than ever. There was something wistful about the way he said it, though, and a friend who visited him after he'd been on his back for nearly six weeks remembered that Howie turned his head quickly into the pillow and began coughing to cover his emotion.

On the night of March 8, 1937, he could stand the confinement no longer. Heaving his leg in its plaster cast, he forced himself upright, took one faltering step, then slowly crumpled to the floor. He was dead. The death certificate said the cause was "a cardiac deficiency and acute excitement." Complicated, perhaps, by a broken heart.

When Howie Morenz died, something died in the Millionaires. It was a strangely quiet crowd that watched the game the night after he died. The Canadiens were prepared to cancel it but Morenz's widow telephoned the Forum in the afternoon. "Don't call it off," she whispered. "He wouldn't want that."

On March 11 the body of Howie Morenz was placed at center ice in the Forum, and Canadien players formed an honor guard as thousands filed past. Fifteen thousand people moved slowly and silently into the Forum for the service, and 25,000 more with heads bared packed the streets outside. Thousands more lined the long route to the cemetery up the snow-covered slopes of Mount Royal. The casket was covered with a huge floral "7." It was the final tribute of his teammates. No Canadien player has ever again worn that number.

BOBBY ORR

[1948–   ]

Is there a real Bobby Orr or did someone compose a giant myth?

Nothing in the history of professional hockey can match the story of the child defenseman who joined the Boston Bruins in the autumn of 1966 and instantly became a star at eighteen. By the end of his second season, and not quite twenty, Bobby Orr was clearly acknowledged as the best defenseman in hockey. During his fifth season, and not yet twenty-three, he was elected by *Sports Illustrated* magazine as Sportsman of the Year and called "the greatest player ever to don skates; not the greatest defenseman, the greatest player at either end of the ice." And by the end of his sixth season, and just turned twenty-four, it was almost necessary to write one record book for him and one for the rest of the players in the NHL.

In Orr's first six seasons he had:

● won the Calder Trophy as the league's outstanding rookie

● won the Hart Trophy as the league's most valuable player three times in succession, the first time anybody had done that in the trophy's forty-nine year history

- been selected on the NHL's First All-Star team five times in succession (he was selected on the Second Team in his rookie year)
- won the James Norris Trophy as the league's best defenseman five times
- won the Smythe Trophy as the outstanding player in the Stanley Cup playoffs (he did it twice)
- set a record for goals by a defenseman in a single season, 37 (he did that twice, too)
- set a record for assists by *any*body in a single season, 102
- set a record for points by a defenseman in a single season, 139
- set a record for points by a defenseman in the playoffs, 24
- set a record for assists by *any*body in the playoffs, 19

Orr's marvellous offensive skills, his remarkable puck control, instant acceleration and, above all, his fearless drive through narrow openings took their toll during those first six years. He underwent major surgery three times in that period for an assortment of ligament and tendon repair on both knees, and there was genuine fear in the autumn of 1972 that his abilities might be permanently impaired in the wake of remedial surgery the previous June after he'd led Boston to its second Stanley Cup championship in three years. Three months after the operation Orr went overseas with Team Canada, a collection of NHL all-stars, for the second half of an historic eight-game series with the Russian national team. He skated in practice sessions in Stockholm and Moscow, but after each workout his right knee swelled and was so excessively painful that he was unable to play in a series that caught up all of Canada and most of the U.S.S.R.

(the games were televised throughout both countries) in a fever of excitement and, in Canada's case at least, an incredible outpouring of nationalism. Canada won the final three games, the last by 6–5 on a goal by Paul Henderson with thirty-four seconds of playing time remaining, to win an emotionally exhausting series by four games to three, with one tie. Back home, Orr's slow-mending knee caused growing alarm until December as the Bruins struggled fitfully in the middle of the standings. When he finally rejoined the team, though, he once again provided the spark he had been generating ever since he was a fourteen-year-old youngster in Parry Sound, Ontario, and within weeks the Bruins were back near the top of the standings, battling Montreal and New York.

It was ironic that the Bruin saga in signing Bobby Orr in the first place related mainly to Wren Blair, a brisk, intense, vigorous young veteran of numerous hockey jobs who became coach and general manager of the Minnesota North Stars in 1967 when expansion brought that team and five others into the NHL. That was one year after Orr had made his debut with the Bruins largely because of the persistence of Blair, and of course Blair, like every other non-Boston employee, suffered Orr's skills ever after. Blair first saw Orr when Bobby was twelve. The boy was playing for the Parry Sound bantams who traveled to Gananoque, a little town on the St. Lawrence River midway between Toronto and Montreal. This was in the spring of 1960 and Blair, general manager and coach of a Boston-sponsored professional team near Gananoque—the Kingston Frontenacs—often watched minor hockey teams in his spare moments. He'd been following a couple of Gananoque kids, and he invited Lynn Patrick, then general manager of the Bruins, to give his appraisal of them in this playoff series with Parry Sound.

Toward the end of the first period, Blair turned to Patrick. "Do you see what I see?" he asked.

"I see what you see," replied Patrick. "Who is he?"

"You got me," said Blair, shaking his head.

He moved off to enquire. When he returned, he told Patrick, "That number 2 we're watching is named Bobby Orr." And then he added in mounting excitement, "Nobody's sponsoring them."

These were three vital words. What they meant was that no professional team held sponsorship rights in the Parry Sound area. Thus, no professional team had a claim on the players.

In the ensuing two years, Blair haunted the Parry Sound area, visiting the Orr family there at every opportunity. Bobby, he soon learned, was the third of five children of Doug and Arva Orr, living in the beautiful little town of Parry Sound, 140 miles north of Toronto on Georgian Bay. In 1960 when Blair first met the family after seeing twelve-year-old Bobby, the two Orr girls, Pat and Penny, were fifteen and nine, and the other two boys, Ron and Doug, were fourteen and six. Bobby's father Doug was a lean, tall, crew-cut, gregarious, sports-loving man of thirty-five, born and bred in Parry Sound and a hockey player there in his youth. Arva, Bobby's mother, struck Blair as being a forthright woman with a strong will, a level eye, and a plain-spoken pride in her brood. At that time whenever she watched her sons play hockey, it was almost impossible to curb her.

"I try to let on I'm not with her," Bobby's sister Pat used to say with a smile of her mother. "Let's say she's unrestrained."

Nor did Arva like sitting with her husband at hockey

games. "Doug sits me down too often," she'd complain.

Doug's married sister, Marg Atherton, was equally unfettered. Once at a game in St. Catharines after Bobby had gone to play junior hockey for the Oshawa Generals, a hometown player, Chuck Kelly, got in a fight with Bobby near Marg's seat. "You brute!" Marg cried, reaching toward Kelly and actually planting a punch on his forehead. "Don't you dare hit Bobby!"

Doug Orr worked for Canadian Industries Limited in the early 1960s, packing high explosives five days a week and watching the Oshawa team on car trips to junior towns on weekends. The youngest boy, Dougie, was horrified when Bobby first entered the Bruin system as a junior. "I'll cheer for Toronto until Bobby turns pro," he'd say gravely, "and then I guess I'll have to switch."

Young Dougie was not alone, of course, in wondering why Bobby selected the then battered Bruins who had taken up virtually permanent possession of the NHL's nether regions. But the player himself, even at fourteen when he finally made the decision to accept Wren Blair's Boston affiliation, showed a precocious business sense. "They need players," he noted to his dad. In other words, the top clubs were well stocked; the road to a regular berth was longer. As it turned out, of course, Orr could have gone to *any* club and become a star; at fourteen he was looking for the short route.

But in those first two years after he'd seen the child, Wren Blair beat a steady tattoo on the door of the Orrs' big, comfortably old stucco house to advance the advantages of Boston. To enhance Bruin prestige in Parry Sound, the NHL club paid a thousand dollars a year for three years toward minor hockey there. In the autumn of 1962 Blair persuaded Arva and Doug Orr to let their fourteen-year-old son attend a Boston junior tryout camp at Niagara Falls. He had been growing fearful that some other NHL club would induce the boy's parents to let him move to a town whose team it sponsored, thus acquiring the rights Blair had so long pursued.

"We had about seventy players at the Niagara Falls camp," Blair once recalled, "and the kid was a stickout. My wife Elma and I drove immediately to Parry Sound to convince the Orrs that Bobby ought to move to Oshawa and sign a junior card with the Generals. Then we'd have him, and my worries would be over."

The Orrs were reluctant. All through a Saturday evening Blair talked to Bobby's father, but though Doug was beginning to bend he wouldn't break. Through Sunday Blair cajoled and implored. It wasn't a matter of money; it was purely that the Orrs were too close-knit a family to feel that their fourteen-year-old was ready to leave the nest.

"Mr. Blair," Arva said over and over, "he's just too young." Once, she added, "Next year, I promise you, he'll go. But not yet."

"I'll find a fine family for him to live with in Oshawa," countered Blair. "He'll get the best of care. If he stays here another year he'll just deterioriate as a hockey player. He's too good for these boys. He'll just learn bad habits."

And then Blair had an inspiration.

"Just let him come on a four-game trial basis," he suggested. "You come with him. See the school. See the folks he'll live with. Watch him play. If you're not convinced after four games, we'll forget it."

So they went.

After four games, and some relatively modest financial arrangements, the Orrs relented, with the stipulation that instead of moving to Oshawa Bobby would commute.

And so he did. Two or three nights a week and on Sunday afternoons, the Orrs or friends of the family drove Bobby 150 miles south for games and 150 miles north after them, through snowstroms sometimes, and sleet and rain.

"Imagine," marvelled Blair later, ignoring the discomfiture of the adults, "the kid never once practiced with the club and he made the second all-star team in the best junior hockey league in Canada."

When he was fifteen, Bobby moved to Oshawa where he lived in a neat modern red-brick bungalow with Mr. and Mrs. Jack Wild. He scored three goals in the second-last game of that season for a total of thirty goals in the fifty-six game schedule, which beat the old league scoring record for defensemen established by Jacques Laperriere—who later joined the Montreal Canadiens—when Laperriere was nineteen. And young Orr attained a 71.3 percent average in passing Grade 9. He kept in frequent touch with the family and sometimes hitchhiked from Oshawa to Parry Sound to visit.

"We're a nutty family," Bobby's sister Pat reflected at that time. "We've all got wild tempers but we're soft as mush, too. Every time Bobby phones I cry and I can hear him start to blubber, too. I always cry when I see him. Dad thinks we're nuts; we'll all be watching a television program, and I look over to see if Mom's crying, and she is, and she looks at me and we both look at Penny and we're all sitting there sobbing away. Dad looks at us and just shakes his head."

In the off-season after he turned sixteen, Bobby did what he could to improve his NHL chances. He worked on barbells twice a day for forty-five minutes, and carried a set of handgrips with him which he squeezed by the hour to strengthen his big wrists and forearms. He ran twice around the harbor every day—two miles a trip. He picked up what money he could, too. When he was thirteen he was a bellboy at a dollar a day in the Belvedere Hotel, which later burned down, and earned $500 in tips. When he was fourteen, after the hotel burned, he got $10 a month from the school board for being the caretaker's helper after school, cleaning out furnaces and shinnying up and down narrow flues to clean them. At fifteen, he spent the summer working in his uncle's butcher shop for $25 a week and all the steaks he could eat. The following summer he made $35 a week as a clerk in Adams Men's Wear in Parry Sound.

At this stage of Orr's development, the Bruins could merely sit and hope the fates had equipped him with an intangible urge to rise with fire in his eyes after some hulking NHL defenseman had flattened him. Or that nature had provided him with the physique required to withstand NHL punishment—as a junior, Bobby was a slender five-foot-nine and 165 pounds. And there were other intangibles.

For instance, as Wren Blair pointed out at that period, a hockey player is a unique athlete.

"A hockey player," Wren said, "can play all games well, but few stars of another sport can play hockey at all. Can you imagine Joe Namath or Arnold Palmer or Muhammad Ali or Johnny Bench able to make even a school hockey team? Yet Gordie Howe used to work out regularly with the Detroit Tigers, and when Jim Norris promoted all the big fights and owned the Detroit Red Wings he'd look at Howe stripped down in the dressing room and he'd say, 'Gordie, with a build like that you could be the heavyweight champion of the world.' Any number of hockey players can hit a golf ball as far as most pros; in fact, a lot of them *are* pros in the off-season.

"The point is, every hockey player must have the attributes of the top athletes in any game, except they must then add the encumbrance of skates. We grow up taking these things for granted in Canada, but the truth is that hockey is the most difficult of all games to master."

But, as it turned out, of course, Bruins' fears were groundless. Nature lifted Bobby Orr to five-feet-eleven and put 190 pounds of tough meat together. And, perhaps because of the nature of the family he came from, he never lost the sense of his own worth or the ability to keep all of his accomplishments in perspective. If he ever grew weary of the youngsters endlessly hounding him for a word or an autograph, or tired of countless visits to hospitals he made privately to cheer old people and young alike, he gave no sign. He tried to keep those visits secrets from the media, but Jack Olsen, writing about him in *Sports Illustrated,* after the magazine had named him Sportsman of the Year, prodded this observation from him about them: "Okay, I'm lucky, right? I've been gifted, right? But the world is full of people who've not been gifted. Not only haven't they been gifted, but they've had things taken away from them. All I have to do is see one of them; some little girl who can't walk, and then I don't feel like such a big hero any more. I think that compared to those people I'm a very small article."

He was nobody's patsy, financially or otherwise. Starving as they were for his skills when Orr finally turned eighteen and became eligible to play in the NHL, the Bruins began negotiations with him as though he were some sore-armed third-baseman cast off by the Red Sox. They offered him a $5000 bonus to sign a two-year contract at $7500 for the first season and $8000 for the second. Doug Orr, Bobby's father, sought out a Toronto lawyer of his acquaintance, a lacrosse player who'd just hung out his shingle. His name was Robert Alan Eagleson, and what Robert Alan Eagleson accomplished with the Boston management on behalf of Bobby Orr revolutionized the world of professional hockey.

Eagleson readily recognized that the management of those recent dreadful Boston teams was in no position to haggle over the most sensational junior since Bobby Hull. He negotiated an $85,000 two-year contract for Orr—more than four times the original Boston offer.

"He was worth every dime," Eagleson pointed out toward the end of Orr's first season in the spring of 1967. "Boston hockey writers told me that by Christmas the kid had increased Bruin attendance by $100,000."

And when that contract expired, Eagleson negotiated another for five years—this one at a flat $1,000,000—and handled Orr's investments, endorsements, and business ventures outside hockey so successfully that he was able to chuckle one afternoon riding a sight-seeing boat across the canals of Stockholm as Team Canada prepared for its Russian invasion, "Well, it took a little longer than I thought to turn Bobby into a millionaire. I figured we'd do it in five years, but we needed a few months more than that."

But it wasn't only Bobby Orr who benefited from Doug Orr's call to Eagleson, and it was not the lawyer's maneuvering with the Boston management that alone revolutionized the structure of hockey, although it had a direct bearing on it. The eruption began in Springfield, Mass., where the legendary Eddie Shore owned the Springfield Indians of the American Hockey League. The situation there had long been a very bad joke in hockey, largely unpublished out of deference, apparently, to Shore's stature as an all-time great player. But he ran his hockey players in Springfield with the overtones of a Captain Queeg, and no one ever raised a hand against him except the players whose faint cries were always unheeded by the game's governors.

Shore often made goalkeepers practice six hours a day in an *empty* rink, diving around the net in full equipment, making imaginary saves from nonexistent attackers. He'd spy on them from the far reaches of the rink and if they stopped to rest he'd roar at them. They got a half-hour break at noon to clomp across the street to a lunchcounter, in full gear. Finally, midway through the 1966–67 season, the players told Shore they were through playing hockey unless he gave them proper working conditions. He refused to alter his antiquated inflexible methods.

Aware of Eagleson's success in bargaining with Boston on behalf of Orr, the Springfield players decided to ask him to represent them. One of them telephoned him in his Toronto office.

"How about the league president?" the lawyer asked. "Why don't you consult him?"

"We did," the player told him. "He said if we aren't on the ice tomorrow morning we'll be black-balled and never play hockey again."

Later, Eagleson recalled: "That's when I blew my top. I went to Springfield. And then it turned out that the league president, Jack Butterfield, was Shore's nephew!"

Eagleson held his meeting with the Springfield players in a hotel room where they listed their complaints.

"When you hear one Shore story you smile, as people seem to have been doing for years," Eagleson later recounted grimly. "When you hear ten you might still grin weakly. When you hear a hundred—and there *are* a hundred—you want to throw up. If the players were dogs you'd pick up the phone and call the Humane Society."

In lengthy negotiation filled with critical moments, Eagleson was able to settle the Springfield situation by getting Shore to stop interfering with his coach in the handling of players, and even to abandon his role as medical diagnostician of his players' various ills, which he adopted from time to time. Eagleson's major weapon was the threat of challenging the players' working conditions in a court of law.

The Springfield settlement, along with Eagleson's handling of Orr, triggered formation of the National Hockey League Players' Association, which made hockey history. NHL front offices for years resisted occasional timid forays from the servants' quarters. In 1957 a majority of big-league players was brought into concord by a New York attorney, Milton Mound, but it was an uneasy alliance quickly dissipated by such kindly old reactionaries as Conn Smythe of Toronto and Jack Adams of Detroit. Adams table-thumped most of his players into a public disavowal of association allegiance. Without Detroit, the union collapsed. Three ringleaders, Ted Lindsay of Detroit and Jimmy Thomson and Tod Sloan of Toronto, found themselves traded to what passed for purgatory in those days—Chicago. This was a coincidence that discouraged serious union involvement for a decade—until Eagleson came along armed with the greatest hockey player of the century and a solution to the Springfield mess.

One December day in 1966 he was lunching with Orr before a Bruin game in Montreal. Two Boston players approached their table and invited Eagleson to Orr's hotel room. When he arrived he found the room filled with Boston players. They asked him about the possibility of forming a players' association. By then Eagleson had at least one client on each of the six NHL teams and through them he sounded out the rest of the players. He drew up a pledge, had it mimeographed, and circulated it through his clients. This pledge read: "I, the undersigned, hereby direct and authorize R. Alan Eagleson to act as my agent in pursuing the formation of a Players' Association for Professional Hockey. It is further understood and agreed that my name will not be used or released in any way without my written consent."

Eagleson said later that he advised NHL President Clarence Campbell two weeks before the June 7 meeting at which he scored his coup that he had pledges from virtually all NHL players and that he'd seek recognition for the association.

"And yet, many owners apparently wouldn't believe it," he said. "The night before the meeting Sam Pollock, the general manager at Montreal, was convinced that none of his players had signed with us. In point of fact, only four hadn't, and only because they'd missed my meeting with Canadien players; they'd told me they'd sign."

The union took the players from peak to peak in altitudes they'd only dreamed of, and when expansion came Eagleson had the new players safely in the fold, too. And he and Orr climbed even higher as partners in a business relationship which as he said that day on the canals of Stockholm made Orr a millionaire while he was still a young man of twenty-four. Between the two of them they revolutionized the game —one of them off the ice, the other on.

During his early years in the NHL, while he was still a teenager, Orr often seemed more like an invention than a real live boy. He was polite, good-natured, relaxed, modest, generous, thoughtful, adjusted; he had an occasional glass of beer with his teammates after a game, he was never uptight as so many kids seemed to be in the generation of the restless hippies (remember *that* old word?), he wore a crewcut, for God's sake, the players liked him, his siblings adored him, kids modelled themselves after him. And, as far as anyone could make out, he had assimilated all the pressures, prophecies, and fanfares that presaged and accompanied his arrival into professional hockey with poise and amiable grace. After six years in the league, not much had changed, except that his hair was mod and his clothes magnificently tailored and though his knees were wonky he was still a strong, effortless skater with instant acceleration that hurtled him towards an opening when he sensed one, or gave him a step that sprung him free of a frantically backtracking defenseman if he got a break. He still had an instinctive sense of how to build a play, a certain feel of how an offensive maneuver could develop. He was still polite, good-natured, relaxed, modest, generous, thoughtful, adjusted, though of course fame and fortune had matured him, and of him it was still possible to say: Is there a real Bobby Orr or did someone compose a giant myth?

LORNE (GUMP) WORSLEY

[1929–   ]

It WAS NEVER easy to take Gump Worsley seriously as an athlete. Through all of his twenty years as a big-league goaltender he was lumpy and stumpy and wore a pot on him like a tame bee. Even Toe Blake, hockey's most successful coach, didn't realize back in June 1963 how much goaltender he was getting when Gump joined Blake's Montreal Canadiens in a seven-man trade with the New York Rangers. Gump was an old guy of thirty-four then, a worn runt, and Blake's main motivation in making the trade was to unload the incumbent goaler, Jacques Plante, a celebrated hypochondriac and dressing room malcontent for years in Montreal. So it wasn't even late-blooming recognition by Blake that rescued Worsley from more than a decade in the New York shooting gallery and similar purgatorial ice patches in Springfield, Providence, Saskatoon, New Haven, St. Paul, Vancouver, and Quebec City.

But soon Worsley was taken very serious indeed, especially by Blake. By the time Gump was thirty-nine—and some mornings feeling ninety-three—he had backstopped the Canadiens to four Stanley Cup triumphs in five years and in the spring of 1966, for the first time in his nomadic life, and again in 1968, he had won the Vezina Trophy as the NHL's top goaltender. And by February 1970 at age forty he was undertaking a new lease on life with the Minnesota North Stars for whom he toiled with vigor, honor, and a certain insouciance until early 1973 when he finally hung up his tack after a professional career stretching all the way back to 1949.

Gump traveled a long, long way. Even in 1964 he was no longer a big-leaguer a year after he was sprung from the Rangers and had joined the Canadiens. He spent the season on the Montreal farm club at Quebec City; and when the annual league draft of players came along in June, the Canadiens decided to leave Gump unprotected. He was available for $20,000 in those days before the league expanded, and none of Montreal's rivals wanted him in the old six-team NHL.

So he was washed up, apparently, expendable to the champions, unwanted by the rest. He was pegged as a jolly, jowly journeyman closing out a career principally noted for his heroics with the Rangers and for ripostes involving Phil Watson, a profane and volatile Ranger coach for five seasons during the latter half of the 1950s. In the most celebrated of these exchanges, Watson was alibiing a five-game losing streak for the benefit of Garden hockey writers.

"I got a beer-belly in goal, and the rest of these bastards just aren't in shape," said Watson, whose voice rose an octave whenever he was agitated.

Worsley was philosophical when his comment was sought.

"Watson is full of baloney," he remarked. "I never drink beer, and he knows it." He tapped an ash from a cigarette. "Only whisky."

One early fall, the Rangers played a pre-season game in

New Haven, and because of excessively warm weather the ice surface became blanketed by fog. In the dressing room after the second period Watson encountered Gump unconcernedly removing his equipment. As Watson's voice began to rise, Worsley cut in:

"I can't see in that soup," he said casually. "so I'm quitting for the night. I'm far too valuable a man to risk injury in a game that means nothing." He put on his clothes and left.

During Gump's decade with the Rangers it wasn't unusual for him to be pelted by fifty or more shots when the enemy was the whirling Habitants of Montreal, or when he faced the more deliberate firepower of Bobby Hull and his pals on the Chicago Black Hawks. Worsley was once asked which team gave him the most trouble in the New York cage.

"The Rangers," he said, civilly.

And then, one bright June afternoon in 1963 it all changed. Gump was basking in the backyard of his Montreal home nursing a small hangover honorably acquired the night before with his boss, Muzz Patrick, then the Ranger general manager. It was the eve of the annual draft meetings at the Mount Royal Hotel and trade talk wafted on the air thick with smoke and lies.

"Are you gonna trade me?" Gump grinned.

"Are you kidding'?" snorted Patrick. "You're a fixture in New York."

"If you ever trade me," mused Gump, "make it Montreal."

And then shortly after noon the next day, a neighbor burst upon Gump's reverie, informing him he'd been traded.

"He had to tell me three times," Worsley recalled later. "Why the hell would I believe him? But it's on the radio every fifteen minutes because it's such a big trade, eh? Me and Dave Balon and Leon Rochefort and Lennie Ronson are coming to Montreal for Plante, Phil Goyette and Donnie Marshall. Now I got to believe it."

What he also got was oblivion. In his eighth game of the new season Gump made a back flip for a sliding puck, pulled a hamstring muscle, and was out for two weeks. When he was ready to play again his job belonged to Charlie Hodge, a slender little veteran four years younger who'd played in Plante's shadow since 1955, usually in the hinterland. So when Gump's leg had mended Blake, the coach, declined to dislodge hot Hodge, who went on to win the Vezina Trophy. Worsley was exiled to the Quebec Aces, Montreal's farm club in the American League, and he was there when the 1964 season opened as well. Hodge, the trophy winner, was still in charge of the big team's cage, and for the umpteenth time in Gump's hockey life he was parted from his wife Doreen and three children, who stayed at home.

But he never lost his sense of style. Once, when he filled in for the injured Hodge for a couple of games, the Quebec Aces won three in a row without him. "What does this mean?" a reporter goaded.

"Omaha," cracked Gump, naming a lower Canadien farm in the Central league.

The wear and tear began to tell on Hodge as the season wore along, and Gump was back for longer periods as Charlie rested. By spring 1965 he was sharing the job with Hodge through a Stanley Cup triumph, and the next season, now thirty-six, he won the job outright, earning the Vezina Trophy, backstopping another Stanley Cup victory and completing one of the more remarkable sports comebacks. Indeed, in the summer of 1967 when the NHL expanded, Hodge went to the obscurity and lassitude of Oakland and a promising youngster, Gary Bauman, to Pittsburgh. The Canadiens strung along with Gump the lump, and young Rogatien Vachon to mind their goal.

It was a wise move. In the 1967–68 season Gump again got his name on the Vezina, playing forty games in the first season of expansion and yielding only seventy-three goals for the league's best goals-against average, 1.98. He had six shutouts and he played every one of the thirteen games the Canadiens required to brush past Boston, Chicago, and St. Louis and win the Stanley Cup. A year later he and Vachon took charge during another championship season for the Montrealers. He played thirty games and got five shutouts.

By New Year's Day 1970, though, it seemed Gump surely was through. Vachon played game after game and, indeed, Gump had started only six times. At forty, he appeared finally to have run his race. But then Wren Blair, the general manager at Minnesota, convinced that Worsley was what the young North Stars needed as a stabilizer, swung a deal with the Canadiens whereby Gump moved over to the West Division. He finished out that season, played two more years sharing the goaltending duties with Cesare Maniago, and was into a fourth year at Minnesota when he decided finally in January 1973, just four moths short of his forty-fourth birthday, that he'd had enough hockey, and particularly enough of the airplane travel he'd always loathed.

Curiously, the most difficult time of Gump's long career, though it was by far the most productive, was his five-year tenure in Montreal. He once confessed that it was harder to play there with a winner than, say, in New York with a chronic loser.

"For one single reason," he expanded, forcefully, "in Montreal, you *got* to win. The pressure there is always heavy on your head."

Late one August afternoon just before training camp opened, Gump was sitting with a friend in a little coffee joint on Peel Street in Montreal, and kids, young men, and old guys steering kids kept coming to the booth to get his autograph. Two dark-haired girls in the next booth looked silently at him, talking quietly to each other for short moments, then returning their long impassive glances to him. He was oblivious of them, sipping coffee, chain-smoking cigarettes, talking earnestly, waving his hands to emphasize points, a stocky little man with a big rounded upper body, heavy jowls, and his hair low and flat across his forehead from a part on the left side. His thick arched eyebrows created an expression of eternal surprise. Though he was christened Lorne John, kids called him Gump long before he reached his teens, naming him for a comic-strip character, Andy Gump, a chinless fellow he may have resembled then but certainly didn't in later life when his chin grew fatter than an English heavyweight's and blue as 5 o'clock shadow.

Gump, a Montreal native, was born in May 1929—the year that tilted the North American economy. He scratched his way on his hockey skill out of the tough, workingman's suburb of Point St. Charles. His father Bill, a Scot, was an ironworker who had two boys and a girl and didn't work for four years during the Depression. When Gump hit his peak again in Montreal in the latter 1960s, he made a pilgrimage nearly every week back to Point St. Charles to visit old pals —"the ones who aren't in jail"—in a neighborhood pool hall, guys like Alex Neale, a beer waiter at the Sportsman's Tavern. "They like to shoot the breeze," Gump said of these trips. He was making more than $30,000 at the time—he doubled that figure later when expansion inflated the market and took him to Minnesota—but he still went back. "He's a helluva guy," Alex Neale said of him once. "Gump never forgot nobody."

Blowing in his coffee this day on Peel Street, Gump was talking about Montreal. "In this town," he repeated, "you've *got* to win, eh?" He had the Quebecker's speech habit of putting the word "eh," with a question mark, at the end of positive statements. "With the Rangers, if we went on the road and were two and two, that was one hell of a road trip, eh? In Montreal, unless you're three and one on the road, or four and oh, they want to know what's going on. '*We lost two in a row!*' You'd think it was the end of the world, the way these fans react. You remember the spring we lost the first two games of the Stanley Cup final to Detroit here at the Forum? Spring of '65, I think it was, or '66. Anyway, I'm tellin' you, there weren't ten people in this town who figured we had a chance after that. Even my own friends out where I live, this little place east of Montreal, Beloeil, they had us *buried*."

But in other ways, it was magnificent to be in Montreal.

"You look forward to going to the rink, eh? You like the way the guys hang together. I mean, you don't hear guys bitchin' at guys in the dressing room. The big stars are all part of the team, you understand me? Like Jean Beliveau, there's a big man, eh? When we're on the road Jean (when English-speaking players on the Canadiens say Jean it comes out John) says, 'Let's *all* go,' and he means that everybody goes out some place together after a game. I mean, it's *en masse*. It's not the big stars in their clique, and the lesser guys to find their own way; it's *every*body."

It was natural to ask about Toe Blake, what he had contributed, this grim-visaged black-haired veteran coach who retired after the 1967–68 season of triumph. Blake rolled up eight Stanley Cup victories in thirteen years as a thinker after thirteen seasons as a digging, relentless leftwinger somewhat overshadowed by his rightwinger linemate, Rocket Richard.

"This man loved to win, eh?" Worsley pondered, rubbing his hand across a small boy's head after writing him an autograph. "He communicated this . . . this . . . pride in winning. Some guys can communicate, some guys can't, eh? Toe could. He had a way, like an earnestness, of making you feel that since the idea of this game is to win, you've got to give it your best shot—every game. He blew his stack, sure, but if he had something to say to you he'd call you in, and it'd be private. To be a coach, you've got to be a psychologist, eh? You've got twenty different personalities in that room. Remember Dave Creighton with the Rangers? Hell of a hockey player if you handled him right. But if you yelled at him, he might as well take off his clothes. He'd be scared to make a move. Toe knew his twenty guys. He'd draw you aside and he'd say, 'You're not goin' so good. You're goin' down too much and when you go down you're not gettin' up quick enough. Is there anything on your mind? Things okay at home?' Now, me, I responded to this. I figured here's a guy concerned about me. I dunno how he handled the others, but that's how he handled me.

"Phil Watson when he coached the Rangers and I was there, Phil knew as much hockey as any guy I ever knew. He was a great coach—for the game itself, I mean. But he didn't handle his guys. You'd find out what he thought of you the next day in the papers. What kind of a way is that? He got on me once and I said, 'Hey, wait a minute. I was in this league when you came and I'll be here when you're gone.' Worked out that way, eh?"

Worsley survived more than Watson's expostulations. Beyond untold strains, pulls, and bruises, plus uncounted scores of stitches (he never wore a mask, even after they came to universal recognition and acceptance; in 1973, Gump was the last of the maskless goaltenders in the NHL), he surmounted three specific incidents that might well have ended his career, made him a cripple, or even killed him, and two of these involved the Herculean Bobby Hull.

In 1952 in the Western League with the Vancouver Canucks, Worsley was crashed by a bruising Calgary Stampeder defenseman named Gus Kyle, an ex-Mounted Policeman apparently getting his man, as he stood in the goalmouth. The impact sent Worsley rolling and toppling, all legs, arms, and stick, into the boards of the rink a good forty feet away, knocked unconscious. When he came to in a heap, there was no feeling in his body below the waist. Doctors said he would regain use of his legs eventually, but that his goal-keeping was ended.

"That's a funny feeling, I got news for you, when the doc puts needles in you up to your butt and you feel nuthin'," Gump reflected. "After three days it turned out to be only a pinched nerve in my spine and I went back playin'. I wore a steel-ribbed corset all summer, wonderin' every now and then if maybe I was gonna lose my mobility."

In 1959, then a Ranger, Gump crouched as Bobby Hull flashed clear of defenders and lanced toward him. Gump slid out as Hull feinted, trying to bump the puck loose from Hull's stick, reaching flat out to jar it. Hull's skate cut through Gump's glove, slicing his right hand and severing

43

the tendons. He didn't know about the tendons as he watched the Garden doctor prepare to stitch him. But when the doctor told him to straighten his hand, he couldn't. Then two severed tendons popped up through the blood. He was hospitalized for fifteen days. This time it was his hand they kept poking needles in, with no reaction. When he recovered he went to Springfield to get his timing back.

On March 8, 1965, people who had pondered such questions as what would it be like to be in an elevator if the cables snapped at the fifty-fourth floor got an answer to another poser that might enthral sadists: what happens to a goaltender struck on the head by one of Bobby Hull's slapshots? This night in the Chicago Stadium was sheer ecstasy for the 20,000 Black Hawk fans who blocked the aisles, festooned the balconies and were announced, as usual, as being a crowd of 16,666 to comply with the fire laws. With 28 seconds to play, the Hawks were leading the humbled Habitants 7 to 0. The millennium. Through the air rich in smoke and the sound of cowbells and the din of an insurmountable lead, Hull ripped loose with a forty-footer through a maze of sweaty forms milling in front of Worsley. He never saw the puck. It hit him on the right side of his head and he slumped, unconscious, where he had stood. Suddenly, there was only silence in the vast arena. Trainers, doctors, and players knelt over the inert figure. Then it stirred. Moments later, it hoisted itself erect. A great cheer echoed and re-echoed. Gump shook off the gentle aiding hands. He refused to go to the bench. He played out those final twenty-eight seconds in a constant din of acclaim. When it was over, and he was leaving the ice, he waved to the thousands. He stayed all night in a Chicago hospital, and was released the following day after careful observation. He'd suffered only an ugly bruise.

Really, no one yet knew what might happen if a Hull blast truly caught a goaltender. In Worsley's case, the puck had turned in flight and the flat face of it had struck him; the conceivably lethal edge had been at ninety degrees to his head. But even in the knowledge of what might have happened, Gump refused to wear a mask. He couldn't play his game with one, he insisted. He tried a mask in New York in practice one time and when a high shot came, he ducked.

"Why you duckin'?" asked his solicitous leader Phil Watson. "You got a mask, dummy."

"I *had* a mask, dummy," growled Gump, wrenching if off and throwing it into his cage. "When did I ever duck before?"

So he never wore one again, even in practice.

Nor was he either superstitious or dependent upon other outside forces. "Aside from his reflexes and his eyesight, a goaltender has only two things going for him," Gump philosophized. "The goalposts."

For awhile following his reincarnation in Montreal, it seemed conceivable that the imperturbability he'd shown through his ups and downs for nearly two decades as a professional was beginning to be chinked by the need to win in Montreal. After his second straight success as a Stanley Cup goaltender, he began to feel ill a few weeks after the season ended.

"For ten days I couldn't keep anything down," Gump grumbled, frowning that afternoon in Montreal, absently stirring his coffee. "I didn't get much sleep, either, tossing and turning."

45

Then he brightened. "Aw, it was probably the banquet circuit after we won again," he said. "They really love a winner around this town. I gave my stomach a bad time most nights."

He got up and went out into the sunshine of Peel Street and disappeared down the hill toward St. Catherine Street, the main drag, rubbing his little round pot. In the next three seasons he won two more Stanley Cups.

BOBBY HULL

[1939–   ]

AT HOME, WHEN Bobby Hull loafed in his living room, it was hard to get the picture that here was the Golden Jet, the most dashing and attractive player in hockey for a dozen years and more. On the ice, who could miss Number 9? He was so beautifully right for his game. When Bobby Hull swooped to his left, his right leg crossing high, the motion was as fluid as a bird in flight. When he broke into full stride and shot the puck in a black blur, he'd bring a sudden expectant *"oh-h-h"* from the great crowds. The cry fell to a hush if Hull's shot missed the net or exploded in a roar if he scored.

In fifteen years with the Chicago Black Hawks he scored 604 regular-season goals and sixty-two more in Stanley Cup playoffs, and on five occasions he scored fifty goals or better, a feat that once would have seemed impossible. He even did it three times *before* expansion watered everything down. Then he became the game's first millionaire when the Winnipeg Jets of the new World Hockey Association lured him away from the NHL for the fattest contract since water first froze on the surface of a pond.

Between games he was hard to miss too, even off the ice.

On television he was a dimpled pitchman for hair tonic, rubbing his head with Vitalis and advising you to try it, too, dimple deepening in a shy smile. In *Esquire* his muscles bulged from swimsuits and sweaters and even from socks. In four-color displays for practically suitless swimsuits, there he was in Hawaii on the sands of Waikiki with other big athletes from other big sports, his tawny pelt glistening, his grin caressing some delicious doll wearing delicious skin and a Jantzen that just did make the picture. While in workclothes he extolled a Ford tractor and on radio plugged the firm's sedan. Or, back on television between periods, there he was being interviewed after firing three goals past some hapless goaltender telling the interviewer with a nice warm gratifying smile and a nice warm gratifying touch of humility that it was fine to score those three goals, all right, but, gee whiz, the thing that really matters this year is that the Hawks finished on *top;* or else he was telling him that, yes, he enjoyed being a playing coach in Winnipeg, but, golly, the thing that really matters is that the Jets keep *up there.*

God Almighty, the millions must often have wondered, watching and reading, what *is* this?

What it was was the commercial side of Bobby Hull, but the commercial picture of the game's most flamboyant figure, the Superman of the Sixties and Mr. Moneybags of the Seventies, was a hard one to keep in focus if you saw him at home between games and watched him wander around in his socks, his unbuttoned white shirt trailing outside his pants; or occasionally bury one of his four young sons or his daughter deep against his chest or playfully pile the child into the pillows of a couch, or exchange barbs with his wife Joanne.

Bobby Hull and Joanne and their boys—Bobby, Blake, and Brett, who were 11, 10 and 8 in 1973—lived in a surprisingly modest three-bedroom bungalow in Addison, a working-man's suburb of Chicago, through the 1960s before they embarked for Winnipeg. They had bought the house in 1964 and lived there during the hockey seasons. Joanne had been an ice-show skater, a slim, frank, outspoken girl, blue-eyed and freckled, with auburn hair. She met Bobby in 1962 when her show played Chicago. The boys, whom she called "my mutts," were an enormously energetic handful built along their father's burly lines, all with light-blue eyes and great thatches of hair so blond as to be almost platinum. On windy winter days when they were indoors they roamed across the living-room's royal-blue rug like balls of prairie thistle in a high wind, yelling, crying, laughing, slugging one another, standing parade-ground still for admonition, tearing off, wailing, giggling—in short, boys. Joanne, with the help of a quiet bespectacled girl named Sheila Bourette who lived year-round with the Hulls, grimly battled to maintain law and order with her mutts. She ran the motherly gamut from cajolery to a high-pitched shriek, kissing them, belting them, fawning on them, hauling them apart by the hair, slumping on a couch at the end of a day when the sweet-faced tigers were bathed, had peered—scrubbed, angelic, and pyjama-clad—at *Lassie* and *Walt Disney* in living color in the living-room and had been bedded down and hugged and kissed good-night. *Good night!*

The living-room, always the focal point of the day's action on a Sunday when Dad was home between games, was unpretentious and comfortable. There were two abstract paintings, both done by Joanne's brother, Jim McKay, a university student in California where Joanne was born. The only photograph on the walls in those Chicago days was one of the three oldest boys; baby Brett chewing on the lace of a skate

49

and wearing a hockey helmet bearing his dad's No. 9. Blake and Bobby stood over him in skates under their long pants, wearing Black Hawk sweaters and holding sawed-off hockey sticks. Below the picture was a small table on which stood six trophies and a single framed photograph. You could conclude that this corner of the room represented the distillation, the very essence, of Bobby Hull's existence, this picture of his boys and these trophies he'd earned in the NHL, including two bronze plaques recognizing him as the Hart Trophy winner, the league's most valuable player.

The trophies on the small table were the memorabilia one would expect of the most glamorous hockey player of his time; what was unexpected was the single framed photograph a color picture of a brown-and-white bull, a shaggy low-slung blank-faced hulk which Hull matter-of-factly revealed to be "a Hereford, a *Hardean* Hereford, H-a-r-d-e-a-n. It is named for Hardy and Jean Schroeder, who developed the breed. This one weighs 2200 pounds; he's a two-year-old. The man who owned him before I got him refused an offer of $75,000."

Hull was always a farm boy with a passion for purebred cattle. In 1962 he bought a 600-acre farm near the little eastern Ontario community of Demorestville close by the Bay of Quinte on Lake Ontario where he was born and raised, the oldest boy in a family of eleven, with four older sisters and three younger, and three younger brothers. The sire of this vast close-knit brood, heavy-set shambling Robert, born in 1910, was a mill foreman at the Canada Cement plant at Point Anne while they were growing up in a sand-colored, two-story, stuccoed house provided by the company. Bobby, called Robert by the family, was a mere fourteen when he left home to play hockey for a Hawk sponsored Junior B team in Hespeler, Ontario. His mother, a doting, serene woman, recalled once that when Bobby first left home he was extremely homesick, so in her daily letters she rarely mentioned the family but wrote only of trivia. He told her when he got home briefly once between games, "Gee, Mom, keep those letters coming with nothing in them."

It was to these familiar surroundings that Hull returned at the end of every hockey season, long after he and Joanne were married. For their first summer they bought a beautiful sprawling four-bedroom home on the shore of the bay four miles from the 600-acre farm, and they went there each spring in the succeeding years when hockey ended. Hull and his brother Dennis, six years his junior, who joined the Hawks in the autumn of 1964, stocked the farm with 160 Hereford cattle, seven of them bulls worth $120,000 by Hull's estimate.

"This is likely the best herd in Canada," he noted matter-of-factly once, "and I'd argue it's the best in the world."

On the same afternoon that he made this observation he was also considering buying more property near Oshawa, 220 acres some forty miles east of Toronto on which he would put half his herd, and he discussed the purchase idly with Joanne.

"It's a pile of money," he said, frowning. "They want $150,000 for it."

"I keep telling you, it's because you're Bobby Hull," Joanne said. "Tell them you don't want it; they'll come down."

"Oh, Joanne," he said in some exasperation, "people aren't like that."

"The hell they aren't," she muttered.

Joanne turned to a visitor. "Bob doesn't think anybody

would ever try to take him," she said. "He's too . . . what? Modest? He really does downgrade himself. It's the difference in our upbringing, I think. Bob's dad's way of being an admiring father was to tear him down a little. My family was always praising me. So I give him that; I praise him."

All that day, Hull's mood was calm. Was he always this way at home?

"Yes, I guess so," he said, pondering. "Nothing really bothers me."

"If he doesn't score any goals, he's unbearable," interjected Joanne. "He's not fit to live with. And he knows he's impossible to talk to the day of a game. He just won't admit it."

"Joanne, you imagine things."

"Oh, Bob, nobody dares speak to you the day of a game. You're impossible."

"Well, you bug me." Suddenly he grinned at her.

"Yes, I know, dear," she said, smiling. "But you'll admit I bug you most on game days."

She crossed to him and sat on his knee. "You didn't even kiss me hello at the airport," she said. "I might just as well have been asking for your autograph."

He laughed. The Hawks had arrived at Chicago's O'Hare Field from a five-day road trip that day, an hour and twenty minutes late. Joanne had gone to meet her husband, taking the two oldest boys and leaving the rest with Sheila. Several hundred fans had gone out to meet the plane too, and had waited the extra hour and a half. When Hull stepped through the arrival gate with the other players, mobs of people surged toward him. The others made their way anonymously, or at least unhindered, through the crowds. But Hull was circled by a surging throng. One woman asked him to hold her little girl in his arms while she popped her flash camera. Joanne laughed and called to him, "How does it feel, Bob?" He smiled at her, off in the back of the crowd, and Joanne explained, "He wants a little girl," she said. "Hey, where are my mutts?" Later, Hull got his wish; Joanne gave birth to a baby girl.

Now, she searched for Blake and Bobby. They were in the midst of the crowd, on either side of their father, holding onto his knees, staring up at him as he signed endless scraps of paper, two solemn little guys in blue levis and faded yellow T-shirts impassively waiting for their dad. Hull stood there for eighteen minutes by the clock, writing his name over and over, fixing a smile as now and then a flash bulb exploded.

At length, Joanne was asked, "Doesn't he get sick of it?" She replied without hesitation. "He feels if they're interested enough to stay on, he'll keep signing," she said.

At the airport exit a few of the Hawks were still waiting for transportation when Hull joined them, inquiring if they had rides. He called to a fan he recognized and asked him to give two of the players a lift; he told two others to come with him. They, Joanne, the two boys, and Hull's interviewer jammed into a week-old Plymouth; it had been given to him, he said, by a car dealer who wanted Bobby Hull to be known, or at least seen, as a Plymouth driver. Hull also had a Dodge station wagon then, which a dealer had given him a year earlier, and an Oldsmobile convertible. Later, when he started appearing in advertisements endorsing Ford tractors he was given that company's farm equipment, plus $3500 a year for selling his name to the product.

When he reached his suburban home he had barely cleared the front door when he was out of his shoes, coat, tie, and had opened his shirt. He appeared to be a man who liked familiar things around him, one who was uneasy in strange surroundings. When the swimsuit makers flew him to Hawaii for the Jantzen photographs one summer, he was invited to say for two weeks. There were four or five other professional athletes—football telecaster Frank Gifford, golfer Dave Marr, former halfback Paul Hornung, among others—but when Hull's segment of the shooting was finished in five days he hurried home to his farm. When sports-clothes pictures were made in California he stayed one day, returned home for one day, and went back the next for a TV commitment.

"I come home from everywhere in a hurry," he said quietly. "I don't like big hotels or fancy dining rooms—I'm uneasy in them."

He felt most relaxed, he said, holding a hockey stick or wrestling a calf. When hockey ended, he'd fix fences on the farm, re-seed the meadows, plant corn, oats, and hay, drive tractors, plows, and combines, along with his brother Dennis, his brother-in-law Bill Messer, and a friend, Ralph Richards. In addition to the grazing pastures, they'd work seventy-five acres of oats, and take off 10,000 bales of hay. Hull tattooed calves in the spring, indenting the ears with pincers and applying indelible ink. Spring was the time, too, for supervising the breeding of cattle and—very important to him—watching his kids romp. He'd drive the four miles from his summer home on the bay to the farm by 7:30 every morning, and return in the early evening, a twelve-hour day. His sister Maxine, Bill Messer's wife, handled the noon-time meals for the men and boys.

Through the winters he always worked thoughtfully on his game, then as now. To some it appeared he paced himself, even loafed on the ice at times.

"No," he once argued on this proposition, "it isn't loafing; it's experience. The thing you must never do is waste energy. You pick your spots and you go when you know you have the edge. It's an instinct. You get so that you can anticipate when you should outrace or outbody or outmaneuver. You sense your opening and you react. There's a lot in knowing what you yourself can do. You see an opening and something tells you if you can make it. Being in shape is the most important thing. If your legs aren't going fluently, nothing ever gets co-ordinated."

It was never Hull's nature to talk of outslugging an opponent, and he hated discussing the Stanley Cup playoffs of 1965 when he massaged the Detroit Red Wings—singly, in pairs, and by threes—the way a bulldozer explores stumps. The Hawk management had urged him to throw his weight around, advising its star, who had just won the Lady Byng Trophy as the league's most gentlemanly player, that he would never have picked up two serious knee injuries late in the year if he had played tougher hockey. He'd been hurt, they told him, because in playing what Hull called "pamby" hockey he'd been a sitting duck for board checks that wrenched his knees. By the time the Hawks reached Montreal for the final round against the Canadiens, enough of the sophisticated addicts at the Forum had been exposed through television to Hull's rampage against Detroit to boo him roundly.

This shook Hull, a man who wants to be liked. "It hurt my feelings to be booed in Montreal," he recalled. "It had never happened there, a place where they *know* hockey. So I returned to my own game after the blood-and-thunder style of the Detroit series—outmaneuvering them."

But, by coincidence or otherwise, Hull went out of action again early in the 1966 season with a knee injury. The blow that sidelined him came after he'd started the season at a scoring rate never before known in hockey. He'd scored 15 goals in the first eleven games. But when he was knocked out for five games, it appeared his chance of wiping out the goal-scoring record of fifty he then shared with Rocket Richard and Boom Boom Geoffrion would be permanently thwarted by knee problems. Yet he came back from his early injury to attain an even taller pinnacle; fifty-four goals. And with forty-three assists he established a point-scoring record of ninety-seven. He followed this with fifty-two goals in 1967, forty-four in 1968, and fifty-eight in 1969 to lead goal-scorers for the fourth straight time and seventh time in his first dozen years in the NHL. By the end of his tenure in Chicago he'd scored 604 regular-season goals, trailing only Gordie Howe on the all-time list. Howe got 786 goals in his twenty-five year career.

It's conceivable Hull might have retired from hockey had not the offer that made him a millionaire come along in the summer of 1972 and embarked him on a new career in the WHA.

"Playing is not forever," he noted one evening after he'd put in a dozen years. "I've got no scoring records in mind, no record number of years I want to play. I'm a country boy at heart. If I played fifteen seasons, I'd be in my early thirties and that might be enough."

As it turned out, fifteen was precisely the number of years he put in at Chicago. Then he embarked for Winnipeg as playing coach. But he left an indelible impression upon the game he mastered and the league he dominated for so long, an imprint graphically summarized by Al Laney, a thoughtful New York hockey observer who covered the game for four decades following his introduction to it at the old Madison Square Garden in 1926. Writing for the New York *Herald-Tribune* early in Hull's career, Laney said this about the Golden Jet:

"The plain fact is that any time Hull gets a shot it is a potential goal. He is the most spectacular player in the game and he may be the greatest from this point of view that hockey has ever known, in spite of the fabulous Rocket Richard and Gordie Howe. Hull is a popular figure with the crowds, too, even when he is murdering the home team. There never has been a faster skater or one with stronger leg action. It is very likely that Hull fires the puck faster than any man who ever played the game."

Even deep in his career, Hull wanted to be on the ice every day to skate and to shoot. Using a stick with a pronounced hook in the blade, a model introduced by teammate Stan Mikita, Hull worked on the accuracy of his shooting from long distances and odd angles. The stick enabled him to add a shot to his repertoire in the fashion of baseball pitchers adding a new pitch, and in Hull's case this shot made the puck behave like a knuckleball, with an unpredictable flutter.

"If you don't quite catch all of the puck as you let it go, it'll rise or drop suddenly, depending on the spin," he explained once. "Drawing it toward you as you let it go sets up a different spin and produces a curve."

These refinements did not go entirely unnoticed by Johnny Bower, the ancient Toronto goaltender rounding out a long career. "Hull needs another shot like I need a hole in the head—which I'm apt to get," Bower observed.

However, by the end of the 1970 season the league had

moved to outlaw Hull's knucklers, introducing a rule re-stricting the curvature in stick-blades to one-half inch. This eliminated the trick shots but had no effect on velocity.

It was just as well. If something hadn't been done, Hull might easily have made a prophet out of Bower, and wounding people was never the objective of hockey's Golden Jet.

He changed his life-style somewhat when he and his family moved to Winnipeg, buying a $200,000 home in—obviously—an exclusive neighborhood, and since he was recognized everywhere he went he dressed snappier and was less infor-mal than he'd been in Chicago. But otherwise things didn't change much in the Hull household. Joanne dressed up the living-room and shooed the boys and Bob to the recreation room, but there he playfully roughhoused with the mutts as he'd always done. And since the new home was only a five-minute drive from the Winnipeg Arena he was able to spend more time with his family than he had in Chicago. Things really weren't too different. Except he was richer, with a mil-lion in cash and another million over the next ten years. He could buy all the Hardean Herefords in the world.

MAURICE (ROCKET) RICHARD

[1921–   ]

 $\mathcal{T}$ HERE IS NO question that Maurice (Rocket) Richard was the most spectacular goal-scorer who ever played hockey. For a long time he was the game's greatest scorer, but eventually, as though subjecting Richard's lifetime total of 544 goals to the Chinese water treatment, Gordie Howe overtook him, long after the Rocket had retired. Indeed, Howe continued methodically to plunk pucks into nets until he had played for twenty-five seasons and had scored 786 goals, an indefatigable man of forty-three. By then he had played nearly 1700 games, whereas Richard had decided to call it a career when he was thirty-eight and had played 978 league games.

Richard scored goals from all angles and positions, often carrying defensemen on his back. Sometimes he scored them while lying flat on his back, with at least one defender clutching his stick, another hacking at his ankles with a pair of skates, and a third plucking thoughtfully at his shoulder harness. He was at his peak for the dozen years from 1945 to 1957 when there was a revolution in hockey's cultural standards, a liberalizing process encouraging referees to ignore all but the most flagrant violations of the written rules and, in turn, encouraging poor or indifferent players to cut good or great players down to size by slamming them bodily into the sides of rinks, rubbing their ribs with fiber-encased elbows, inserting sticks between their legs or under their armpits, and generally impeding what once had been considered their lawful progress.

Consequently, the era produced many teams which stood out above their rivals but few individuals who stood out above their peers. For more than a decade in this milieu Richard towered over them all, both as a goal-scorer and as a piece of property. The Montreal Canadiens, for whom he toiled throughout his career, were once offered a lump payment of $135,000 for Richard, the highest value to that point in time ever placed in any kind of serious—or sober —vein upon a single player, and they flatly and instantly refused the bid.

Considering the completeness of his triumph over adverse working conditions, Richard's attitude toward his work was fairly restrained, but there were occasional violent outbursts of Brobdingnagian dimension. However, if Richard reveled in his position as the most esteemed Candian athlete of his generation he never gave sign of it. On the ice, his dark brooding features seldom departed from their melancholy cast except on the occasion of another Richard goal when they would quickly dissolve into a fleeting expression halfway between a glower and a grin. Off the ice, he was monosyllabic and uncommunicative through most of his long career, even among the players he considered his closest friends. "Maurice can relax," his teammate Elmer Lach once said, "but not during the hockey season."

Toward the end of his hockey life—and, indeed, in proportion to his increasing familiarity with the English language—Richard mellowed discernibly, and his previous off-rink gracelessness all but vanished.

Behind this early impassive facade lay deep wells of sentiment, of sensitivity, and of temperament. On an exhibition tour to the west coast he once cried openly when told he would have to accompany the team to California from British Columbia before returning to his family in Montreal. A much more widely publicized display of his temperament occurred in 1951 when he brooded all night over an adverse decision made by referee Hugh McLean during a game in Montreal. The next afternoon when Richard happened to see McLean in the lobby of the Piccadilly Hotel in New York, he rushed the official and tried to punch him. And although he was commonly believed to be indifferent to the hostility or sympathy of spectators, his employers attributed a long and near chronic inability to play well in Toronto's Maple Leaf Gardens to the profane and persistent heckling of a rather small and elderly lady fan.

But neither psychoanalysts nor hockety experts were ever able to explain precisely why Richard—who in action frequently looked uninspired or bored and almost awkward—kept on scoring so many goals under such difficult circumstances. The early years of his career coincided with the end of World War II when the competition was patently inferior (from the retrospect of expansion, perhaps it wasn't all *that* inferior). But when it had again achieved its peak Richard kept right on scoring, and Frank Boucher, the coach of the New York Rangers who had thought Richard might be a wartime wonder, changed his mind sufficiently to call him the most spectacular hockey player he had ever seen. "That includes the greatest I'd ever seen before him, Howie Morenz," said Boucher with some reverence.

Of all the dramatic goals Richard ever scored among his

544, one stood out above all others. Such distinctions usually depend on individual preference or presence, but "the Boston goal" would always receive widespread acknowledgement as being *the* goal. It came in the spring of 1950, eliminated the Bruins from the Stanley Cup playoffs, and moved the Canadiens into the final round. The game was tied 1–1 in the third period, and Richard had taken a deep cut over his left eye. He was hurriedly patched up in the infirmary with a bandage across his forehead and around his head from which blood was seeping, creasing his cheek in a long rusty line to his chin. He returned to the Canadien bench late in the game, took his turn on the ice, and subsequently a moment developed when he was behind his own net cradling the puck on his stick and looking up the ice through the haze and frenzy of the churning Montreal Forum.

He started slowly up the right boards and got past his check, Woody Dumart, by outskating him with a quick little burst that carried him across center ice. At the Boston defense Bill Quackenbush and Bob Armstrong waited grimly, and as Richard came toward them Armstrong, the left defenseman, made a move to pin him. But Richard leaped past Armstrong's lunge, moving deep into Boston territory as Quackenbush came across, forcing him toward the corner, and driving into him there. Yet somehow Richard pushed off Quackenbush, shoving his way along the backboards as the big defenseman recovered and came after him. Richard looked like death—pale, blood trickling down his face, his legs working to get him clear of Quackenbush, the stained bandage on his head pushed to a crazy angle. He sprang from Quackenbush, approached the net along the backboards, and somehow worked his way sharply clear of the boards just as it appeared he'd be forced behind the net. As he came out, the goaltender, Sugar Jim Henry, made a frantic dive at the puck before Richard could shoot, but Richard drew the puck clear of Henry's diving form, took a stride to the front of the net, and tucked the puck into it.

Gallicly handsome and eternally intense, Richard defied the most carefully laid plans to defense him. Hap Day, Toronto coach through the whole decade of the 1940s, once said this was mostly because of Richard's unorthodoxy; even his own mistakes sometimes worked to his benefit. The point was never better illustrated than once slightly past Day's time during the Stanley Cup playoffs of 1951 against the league-champion Red Wings. In each of the early games on Detroit ice, Richard scored overtime goals to win the first for the Canadiens after sixty-one minutes and nine seconds of extra play, and the second after forty-two minutes and twenty seconds of overtime.

"In that second game," the Detroit coach of the era, Tommy Ivan, explained painfully, "our Red Kelly got the puck in our end and was trying to clear ahead to Leo Reise. Richard was caught far out of position and the player he was supposed to be checking was breaking for the other blueline. On our club, we try to teach our men never to let that happen. Anyway, as Kelly cleared the puck it hit Richard on the leg, bounced back into our zone past Kelly, and Richard scurried in to pick it up and score the overtime goal."

By a similar freak of magnetism Richard established his record for goals in a single season (fifty in fifty games during the 1944–45 campaign) which stood unsurpassed until Bobby Hull finally broke it nearly two decades later. By late February that season, Richard had counted forty-three goals and needed but one more to tie the record of Joe Malone, who scored forty-four goals in twenty-two games for the Ca-

63

nadiens in 1918. The tying goal eluded Richard for several contests until one Saturday night when the Canadiens moved into Toronto. Richard was checked heavily as he carried the puck near the Leaf net; knocked down, he was sliding along on his stomach, with the puck out of control, when a Leaf defenseman endeavoring to clear the rolling disk deflected it into the Toronto net. There was nothing the official scorer could do but credit the goal to Richard, since he was the last Canadien player to touch the puck. That ended Richard's brief slump. The next night in Montreal he broke Malone's record and went on to score five more goals before the season expired.

A powerfully built man of five-feet-ten and about 175 pounds at his best playing weight, Maurice (pronounced More-reez) Richard (Ree-shar, with the second syllable emphsized) was a hard man to know. His teammate for many years, Glen Harmon, once said this stemmed from Richard's early inability to handle English. Unable to understand what most strangers (particularly sportswriters on the road) were saying to him, Richard would grunt some incomprehensible reply and turn away. As with most of the Canadien players who joined the team unfamiliar with the language, Richard acquired a good working use of English as the years moved along, but until he became acquainted with people outside Montreal he stayed pretty much to himself, or at least remained uncommunicative. He added weight as his career deepened, but through most of it he was a slender-looking fellow with sleek black hair, black eyes, and a small thin-lipped mouth which gave him a rather surly expression. His roommate on the road, Elmer Lach, once noted that it wasn't unusual for the Rocket (whom most of the players called Rock) to sleep more than twelve hours a day, and per-

HOWIE MORENZ

RED KELLY

Michael Burns

ROCKET RICHARD

Michael Burns

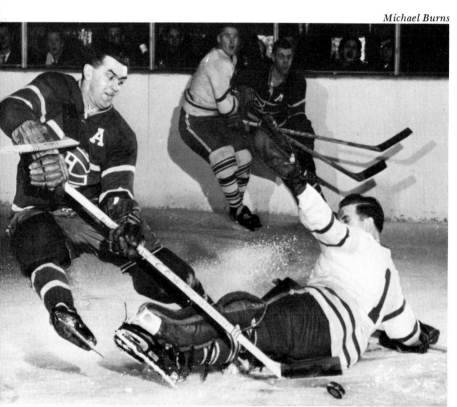

JEAN BELIVEAU

Michael Burns

GUMP WORSLEY

Michael Burns

Michael Burns

TED LINDSAY

Michael Burns

GORDIE HOWE

BOBBY HULL

HENRI RICHARD

PHIL ESPOSITO

BOBBY ORR

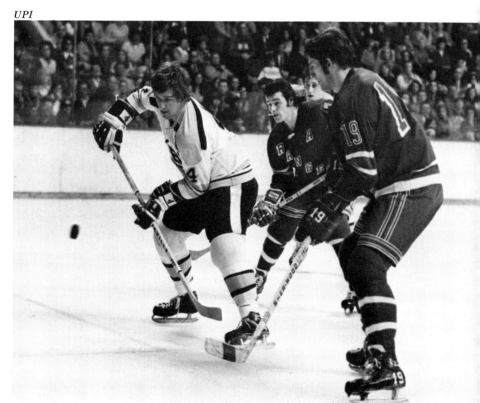

Michael Burns

TERRY SAWCHUK

haps it was from this excessive rest that he derived his vast energy and strength for brief explosive bursts on the ice. Once, driving past a 220-pound defenseman, Earl Seibert, the Rocket bent low to try to avoid a crash. He didn't, and he was staggered as Seibert came barreling across his bent shoulders. When Richard straightened, Seibert was still riding him. Richard took two or three wavering steps to correct his balance, recovered the puck and even faked the goaltender out of position before sweeping the rubber into the net. "I had a better view than the goal judge," lamented Seibert later.

The 1954–55 season was perhaps the most astonishing in Richard's astonishing career, and certainly the most unforgettable. A bizarre series of events began on the night of December 29, 1954, in the Montreal Forum when Richard was involved in a vicious fight with Bob Bailey, a big Toronto rookie. When linesman George Hayes tried to separate them, Richard smashed his empty glove, which he'd tossed aside during the fight, across Hayes's face. Referee Red Storey imposed two misconduct penalties upon Richard, and president Clarence Campbell followed the automatic $50 fine for each of the misconduct penalties with an additional $200 fine for Richard's "gross misconduct" and for his "general flouting of the authority of the officials."

Undeterred, though simmering, Richard seemed bent on winning the scoring championship that season. He had thirty-eight goals and thirty-six assists and was leading the league when the Canadiens engaged in their fourth-to-last game that season against Boston. In the third period Boston's Hal Laycoe highsticked Richard, drawing blood, and the Rock seemed to lose all control. Touching his head and indicating to the referee he'd been cut, he suddenly skated toward Laycoe, swung his stick above his head like an axman, and with both hands struck Laycoe on the shoulder and face.

Linesmen dashed in and got Richard's stick away from him, but he broke free from linesman Cliff Thompson, grabbed a loose stick lying on the ice, and again attacked Laycoe with two one-handed swings across Laycoe's back, breaking the stick. Again Thompson clutched Richard, but again he broke free, found yet another stick, and struck Laycoe a third time across the back as the Bruin ducked. Linesman Thompson wrestled Richard to the ice and held him there until a Canadien player pushed him away. Whereupon Richard leaped to his feet and punched Thompson twice in the face. Referee Frank Udvari, getting order restored at long last, assessed Laycoe a major penalty and gave Richard a match misconduct.

There followed a full investigation by president Campbell who, in a thorough and detailed report of the horrifying scene, concluded: "In the result, Richard will be suspended from all games, both league and playoff, for the balance of the current season."

Campbell could not have created more consternation in Montreal if he had blown up Mayor Jean Drapeau and the entire city hall. The town was stunned, then wrathful. Several anonymous callers pledged to kill the league president.

Two nights later, Detroit went into the Forum tied with the Canadiens for first place, and each team had two games remaining after this one. Campbell and his then secretary and fiancée, Phyllis, who later married him, sat in their box through the first period while fans booed, hissed, and threw eggs as well as assorted debris at them. Then a smoke-bomb exploded nearby. People began to cough and rub their eyes. There was a lull on the ice when the period ended, but pandemonium was building all around it. A hoodlum leaped at Campbell and struck him twice. The police chief escorted Campbell and his fiancée to safety. Then the city fire director, Raymond Pare, ordered the Forum evacuated fearing a panic. When the public-address announcer declared that the game had been forfeited to Detroit an uproar followed. Campbell and his girl were led from the Forum through a side door and driven to safety.

As the crowd dissipated into the streets, people began throwing stones through windows on St. Catherine Street, upsetting cars, roughing up bystanders, and looting. When order returned, damage was estimated at more than $100,-000, and thirty-seven men had been arrested.

Mayor Drapeau appealed to Campbell to stay away from the Saturday night game against New York that followed the Detroit debacle. "His presence could have been interpreted as a real challenge," Drapeau said.

"Challenge?" cried Campbell in rebuttal. "Does the mayor suggest I should have yielded to the intimidation of a few hoodlums?"

The city was still seething, and appeared on the verge of chaos. And then the man around whose head the entire controversy raged, Maurice Richard himself, suggested that he make an appeal to the fans via radio and television. The Canadien dressing room was turned into a studio, cameras and microphones were aimed at the Rocket, and, speaking calmly and with sincerity, he said, first in French, then in English:

"I will take my punishment and come back next year to help the club and the younger players win the Cup. Because I always try so hard to win and had my trouble in Boston, I was suspended. At playoff time it hurts me not to be in the

67

game with my team. However, I want to do what is good for the people of Montreal and my team. So that no further harm will be done, I would like to ask everyone to get behind the team and help the boys to win from Rangers and Detroit."

The city grew calm. Drapeau, Campbell, and the city council plus the fire department and the merchants had failed to bring order but, in the words of sportswriter Andy O'Brien, "the Rocket's sincerity cooled them off as if he'd thrown a bucket of ice water."

The Canadiens also cooled off. They concluded their home season peacefully against the Rangers and went to Detroit the following night to close their schedule. But they lost their last chance to finish on top, bowing to the Red Wings. Detroit beat them in the Stanley Cup final too.

In retrospect, Campbell said he'd had no other choice than to assess Richard the most severe of penalties. The Rocket's attitude toward the officials had grown progressively more hostile and blatant, culminating in his assault on Laycoe and linesman Thompson, whose only sin was trying to dim the Rocket's glare. Richard's attack on referee Hugh McLean in the lobby of the New York hotel was one of the season's most wildly debated episodes. He did this some eighteen hours after a game in which he'd swung on Detroit's Leo Reise who had jeered at him for getting a penalty. Of course, Richard had his own point of view. "A man can take just so much," he said, reconstructing the incident later. "I was skating close to the Detroit net when Sid Abel grabbed me by the chin, nearly twisted my head off, and spun me around. I drew the referee's attention to this. All I said was, 'You must have seen that,' but he laughed in my face. As I skated away I said, 'This is the damnedest thing yet,' and then McLean rushed up and put me off with a misconduct penalty."

When Reise needled him, Richard swung at the Detroit defenseman and drew an additional misconduct penalty from McLean. The next day when Richard encountered McLean and linesman Jim Primeau in the hotel lobby he grabbed McLean by the collar and tried to punch him. He was held by Primeau, who began throwing punches at Richard.

Out of this, Richard was fined $500 by president Campbell who declined to suspend him on the fairly implausible grounds that "the suspension of a great hockey star is not justified if it reflects in the gate receipts. We're trying to conduct a business. If I suspend Richard, a great drawing card wherever he goes, it would affect the attendance of the league." However, Campbell abandoned this strange logic of his following the Boston incident.

A year later, Richard returned to the cauldron of controversy. During a game in New York Ron Murphy of the Rangers swung at Montrealer Boom Boom Geoffrion. He missed. Geoffrion in retaliation whacked Murphy's head with his stick. The blow fractured Murphy's skull and sidelined him for the year. Campbell suspended Geoffrion for all games in which the Canadiens opposed the Rangers and, in Richard's view, that penalty was far too drastic.

In a weekly sports column under Richard's name in the French-language weekly, *Samedi Dimanche,* the Rocket's ghost wrote this column, which Richard authorized:

"If Mr. Campbell wants to throw me out of the league for daring to criticize him, let him do it. Geoffrion is no longer the same since his affair with Murphy. He is demoralized and humiliated for having dared to defend himself against a sneaky and deliberate attack by a third-class player. We know that on numerous occasions President Campbell has rendered decisions against Canadien players. Let Mr. Campbell not try to gain publicity for himself by taking to task a good boy like Boom Boom Geoffrion simply because he is a French-Canadian. If this brings me reprisals, I will step out of hockey, and I know that many other players on the Canadiens will do the same."

What looked like a gravely serious situation was cleverly sidetracked by the careful handling of it by Richard's employer, Frank Selke, the managing director of the Montreal team.

As the Canadiens returned from a road game Selke met the players at the railway terminal and collected three of them, and their wives, and took them to the nearby Windsor Hotel to dinner. It was a convivial group of the Richards, the Geoffrions, and the Ken Mosdells during which there was no discussion of Richard's column. But following dinner, Selke maneuvered himself into a private chat with Maurice.

"I thought you'd be angry with me, Mr. Selke," Richard smiled.

"Maurice," began the tiny Selke, "I've never known you to do a rotten thing. But now you're accusing President Campbell of things that quite probably aren't true. That isn't like Maurice Richard. I doubt that you wrote that column."

"It's true, I didn't, but I did authorize it."

"I am very surprised," said Selke tentatively.

After a pause, he spoke again.

"Mr. Campbell often works very late. He may be across the street in his office now. Why don't we go over there and see?"

Richard was reticent, but at length he agreed.

Campbell was in his office when they arrived, and Richard sat silent for long moments, thinking. Then he said, "I want to apologize, Mr. Campbell. I think it's the decent thing to do. I believe now I have been wrong to have the thoughts I've had."

He wrote an apology in the column too, for which many of the French-language papers accused him of selling out. But not according to a piece by Herbert Warren Wind in *Sports Illustrated*.

"Maurice Richard never disappoints you," Wind quoted Selke. "We have had a lot of dealings. When a mistake is pointed out to him and he sees it as a mistake, he has the character to recognize it and to make genuine rectification. He has great class as a person."

Curiously, the determined Richard seldom exploded in Toronto and it took time to convince that city's fans that Richard was as great as his clippings. The year he got his fifty goals he collected only three—apart from the record-tying one for which he was credited while lying on his stomach—in seven games in Toronto (and there were numerous games over the years at Maple Leaf Gardens when he didn't have even four shots on the net.)

Nor could *he* explain this odd fact. At various times he blamed the heat of the Gardens, its hangar-like interior (there are no posts, no balconies), and the fact that he grew overanxious to succeed in a city he hated. Selke once said Richard detested Toronto because it was typified to him by a woman as abusive as she was well groomed who sat in an expensive seat near the visitors' bench. "She's one of the most foul-mouthed women I've ever heard," Selke said, "and she saves most of it for Maurice."

It must have been the woman; God knows the Toronto team never devised any visible defense for the Rock. At the Forum he found the Toronto net as though he carried a divining rod. Once against them he established a playoff record of five goals in one game. His check that night of March 23, 1944, was Bob Davidson—a tenacious checker—but even Davidson's clutching best wasn't enough to prevent Richard from converting five passes from Toe Blake into records for both of them.

Not surprisingly, considering the adoration that engulfed him in the Forum, Richard was always at his best in Montreal. One night he arrived an hour before game time to tell his coach Dick Irvin he was pooped.

"Pooped?" enquired silver-haired Irvin, "how do you mean, pooped?"

"Moved today," replied the Rock. "Carried furniture up and down stairs all afternoon. I'm beat, pooped."

The Canadiens were playing powerful Detroit that December night, and he moved lethargically onto the ice, and skated as though in a daze through the pre-game warmup. But then Elmer Lach slipped the puck through the defense to Richard who'd somehow acquired the energy to beat his check, so he did what came naturally; he put the puck in the net. Then he scored again. And again. Before the curtain was mercifully lowered around the Detroit net, the pooped Rocket had scored five goals and added three assists in the era of a six-team league when only the best 120 hockey players in the world were regarded as big-leaguers.

Although Richard played for eighteen seasons, he was at his peak during a period of shorter schedules, and he was hurt a great many times, occasionally seriously. Indeed, he played the full schedule only seven times in his eighteen years. Before he became properly established with the Canadiens he broke his left ankle and his left arm, then his right ankle. Over his final three seasons he missed eighty-nine games of the team's 210. In the 1957–58 term, during the fourteenth game, his Achilles tendon was severed in a skate accident and he missed forty-two games. The next year he broke his left tibia near mid-season and didn't get back until the playoffs. And in what turned out to be his final season, 1959–60, he broke a facial bone after twenty games, and missed the following nineteen.

Yet he appeared ready for a nineteenth season of NHL competition when fall training rolled around in September 1960, just after his thirty-ninth birthday. One day, following a routine practice session, he walked into the office of his old linemate who had become the Canadien coach, Toe Blake, and told him that he was through.

It was as simple and as final as that. The most spectacular scorer hockey had ever known had gone to the well often enough. He had no intention of going once too often.

TED LINDSAY

[1 9 2 5 –   ]

STRAIGHT AHEAD was the only direction Ted Lindsay ever traveled in seventeen seasons in the NHL, the last of which was sort of a sentimental postscript in 1964 after he'd retired from the violent ice-ponds in 1960.

Snarling, mocking, richly talented Lindsay spent thirteen tempestuous seasons with the Detroit Red Wings and three more with the Chicago Black Hawks before his first retirement. Four years later at age thirty-nine he came back for another thunderous reunion with the team he always wanted to be identified with, his beloved Red Wings. For nine more years he escaped public attention, and then more people saw him than ever—he turned up as a hockey commentator in two countries just after New Year's 1973 when the National Broadcasting Company and the Canadian Television Network carried an NHL game-of-the-week across the continent, with Lindsay as acerbic and plain-spoken as ever. ("How can the NHL be so low in talent?" he asked one Sunday afternoon, dark eyes glinting and his scarred face twisted in a crooked grin, "that they'd bring Derek Sanderson back from that other league? I mean, I don't blame him for jumping for a ton of money, but a lot of Boston players must have resented it when the Bruins took him back.")

In his own seventeen seasons of pre-expansion turmoil, Lindsay never once observed a detour or saw a stop sign in running up a preposterous 2002 minutes in penalties while becoming one of the highest point-collecting leftwingers of all time, surpassed only by supersonic Bobby Hull. Terrible Ted was something. Lean and built like a middleweight fighter, he took on defensemen who outweighed his 160 by fifty pounds. But while they cut him up and knocked him down they never changed his mind. He once charged the league president, Clarence Campbell, with prejudice. He fought on the ice with his own teammates and off it with fans, cops, and even his longtime employer Jack Adams. In fact, they stopped speaking to each other the year before Lindsay was traded to Chicago.

He even took on the men who owned the league. He did this as president of the Players' Association, a union formed by the serfs in awesome secrecy during a three-month period in the early winter of 1957, with Lindsay as one of its principal instigators and organizers. That union was crushed soon after birth, but it rose again a decade later under the guidance of Toronto lawyer Alan Eagleson. When Lindsay's union's existence was announced by Ted at a New York press conference in February 1957, the owners expressed an astonishment matched only by that of the fans—but for different reasons. The owners were surprised by the gall of the minions who toiled for them; the fans were amazed by the identity of the man the players had named as their president and spokesman: Lindsay, their arch-enemy during working hours.

Lindsay's announcement was made with studied understatement. "We have organized to promote and protect the best interests of the players," he said. "We don't intend to start a revolution. We aren't displeased or discontented about anything right now."

No owner was reassured, especially by those last two words. Conn Smythe of Toronto was so moved by the idea of a union that he called his own team's representative, Jimmy Thomson, "a traitor and a Quisling," according to Thomson. Then Thomson, a Toronto stalwart for twelve seasons, had his contract dispatched by Smythe to the farm club in Rochester. Six months later he was sold to Chicago. So was Lindsay by the unforgiving Adams, known as Jolly Jawn until aroused.

There was a day when Adams loved Terrible Ted like a son. "Lindsay?" he'd beam, "he's my kind of hockey player." If he said it once, he said it a hundred times. Later, explaining why he'd appointed him captain of the Wings, he noted, "Lindsay is captain because Lindsay is a fighter and a leader. He's a player who never quits himself and can stir his team up in the dressing room and on the ice."

But after Lindsay's eleventh season as a Red Wing star—and possibly because the matured Lindsay was showing a lively individuality—the passions faded. Independence of thought was not, Lindsay concluded, a characteristic that was encouraged by NHL executives. "They don't think we have minds of our own," he said once. "They treat us like children."

Whatever his motive, Adams stripped the captain's C from Lindsay's uniform, and then the two stopped speaking to each other. Through his thirteenth season, while Lindsay was enjoying his greatest year, Adams charged him via the newspapers with complacency. Once undismayed by the number of penalties incurred by his tiger, Adams observed of him that "a man can't score from the penalty box." By the time the year ended, one in which Lindsay compiled his own all-time high of eighty-five scoring points and was named for an unprecedented eighth time as the NHL's All-Star leftwinger, the breach was complete. Adams announced that his former untouchable—his own word for a player who would not be sold or traded—was now available. Lindsay told newspapermen that if he were traded he'd quit hockey.

He changed his mind after a series of discussions with James Norris, the Chicago owner, when Detroit sent him to the Hawks. At first he'd been adamant in his decision to retire, but two things led to a reconsideration. "The Chicago club has given me an opportunity that I can't afford to pass up," he said, employing the word opportunity as a euphemism for money. This followed what Lindsay called derogatory statements by Adams about him and his family. He would not then or later expand on the subject. "I'm not going to get into a name-calling exchange with Adams," he explained. "I want the whole thing to blow over. I think Chicago has an up-and-coming club. I'm not sore at Adams. I pity a man like that."

Terrible Ted played it tough during his three seasons with the Hawks; and in the second he led the list of penalized players with a 184-minute total, a career high for him. His conclusion that the once dreadful Hawks were up-and-coming was prophetic: under coach Rudy Pilous they won the Stanley Cup in 1961 for the only time since their formation in 1926.

Lindsay made a career of beating the odds. A boy of nineteen when he joined the Wings in the fall of 1944, he got involved in one of his earliest games with Butch Bouchard, Montreal's block of concrete who outweighed him by fifty-five pounds and was seven inches taller. Bouchard swung his stick as Lindsay skated near him, a reprisal for a surreptitious dig in the ribs, and Lindsay instinctively ducked before he realized that Bouchard's stick was swung low. Instead of hitting him on the thigh or the hip it caught him across the temple. He went to the hospital with a concussion and was under observation for four days. His reaction was typical. "I shouldn't have ducked."

In later years he absorbed a fractured cheekbone, two shoulder separations, so many broken noses that he lost count, and two broken hands. He once estimated that he'd picked up more than 300 stitches, so many of them in his face that his nickname around the league became Little Scarface. But it was no one-way street; he dealt out more than his share of abuse, verbal and physical. He frequently became involved with Bill Ezinicki, a solid rock of a rightwinger for years with Toronto and Boston. They exchanged a few taps, as was their custom, in one such meeting, and suddenly their tempers burst and they began to wood-chop. Then they threw away their sticks and gloves and pummeled one another. Ezinicki needed eleven stitches to close a stick cut from eyebrow to hairline. He needed four more on the side of his head, and four more on the inside of his mouth, where a tooth had been broken off. Lindsay required only one stitch but, not altogether unexpectedly, he needed extended treatment on a badly scarred right hand.

Once, Lindsay damaged Boston's Gerry Toppazzini so severely that Toppazzini refused to permit photographers to take his picture in the hospital. "I don't want my family to see me like this," he said through swollen lips. Sixteen stitches were required to close cuts about his right eye, across his nose, which was broken, and around his mouth. Lindsay insisted the injuries to Toppazzini were accidental. "It was the kind of play that happens dozens of times a season," he commented. "We didn't see each other until the last minute. Then I threw up my hands to protect myself. Somehow my stick hit his face." Toppazzini bore out this version when Lindsay visited his hospital room. "It was an accident, all right," said the battered Bostonian. "It could have been him."

Lindsay, who often said he felt hatred for every opponent during a game, once even hammered a teammate. This was a rookie named Red-Eye Hay, a rambunctious, rough-and-ready young fellow who was playing opposite Lindsay in an intra-squad exhibition game in Sault Ste. Marie. Lindsay remarked later that he'd taken exception to the way Hay was "throwing his weight around against one of our kids." So he went after him, and they fought for fully a minute. Then, in the penalty box, a fan badgered Lindsay and he climbed over the back of the box and took on the fan in the stands. He missed a step, fell down the stairs of an aisle, and when a policeman grabbed him Lindsay started swinging at him too.

At the root of Lindsay's violence was his size—he never played at more than 165 and he was five-feet-eight—and it was his lifetime notion that no man could last in the NHL who ever backed away from a fight.

"A little guy has to have plenty of self-confidence, maybe even seem cocky," he once philosophized. "The first thing they find out in hockey is if you can take it. I had the idea that I should beat up every player I tangled with, and nothing ever convinced me it wasn't a good idea. What are you going to do when some guy gives it to you, skate away? You wouldn't last five games."

Not many performers melded ferocity with skill. Even

Maurice Richard, often regarded as the most tempestuous forward of all time, was nearly 500 minutes behind Lindsay in penalties. Even by 1973, a decade after his retirement, his 1808 penalty minutes in league play (and 194 more in the Stanley Cup playoffs) were well beyond anyone's reach, 165 minutes ahead of runner-up Gordie Howe, Lindsay's longtime linemate. Yet he combined his truculence with great offensive skill, and was named the league's number one leftwinger eight times. As of 1973, with the game having been thrown wide-open by expansion and goals dropping into nets like cod, he was still ninth on the all-time scoring list with 379 goals, and he was ninth in assists, too, with 472.

Lindsay's skill and his combativeness, his scars, his visit to Toppazzini, his refusal to blame big Bouchard for giving him a concussion, his refusal to back away from a fight—all these were keys to the character of the volcanic Lindsay, an unexpectedly calm, personable and even gentle person away from the battle pits. With the small man's compulsion to prove he belongs, he once claimed he hadn't started more than half the brawls in which he'd been embroiled, an assessment the former Toronto defenseman Jim Thomson always claimed to be "at least a modest, not to say ridiculous, exaggeration."

"He's sneaky," Thomson observed during their playing days. "You've got to keep your eyes open all the time or he'll cut your heart out. He can be a fine friendly fellow off the ice, but once they drop that puck, look out. He loves to win."

His wife Pat, a vivacious blue-eyed Detroit girl, once revealed that she and Ted had to stop playing gin rummy and cribbage because he couldn't stand to lose. "He'd get, well, pouty," Pat said. "It just wasn't worth it." When Lindsay and Jim Thomson played junior hockey for the Toronto St. Mike's, they'd while away occasional afternoons playing hearts with teammates Gus Mortson and Bobby Schnurr. Hearts is a game in which the object is to take as few heart tricks as possible and at all costs to avoid taking the queen of spades. Lindsay was trapped into taking the queen six times in one game and although they were playing for only a fiftieth of a cent a point he leaped to his feet the sixth time, grabbed the deck and threw the cards out the window.

He carried that will to win through his hockey career. He was so determined to prove his authority when Jack Adams made him captain of the Red Wings that he set a record for penalties then in a single game—thirty minutes, precisely half the playing time.

That was against Toronto on October 12, 1952, when he roamed all over the ice to stand up for his teammates. He even rushed to the aid of Gordie Howe, four inches taller and thirty pounds heavier and a man who scarcely needed any outside forces to assist him in a fight. Howe was enjoying a routine scrap with Ted Kennedy of the Leafs when Lindsay charged across the ice to earn himself a major penalty. Then he got a second major for fighting with a scrappy little Leaf, Gordie Hannigan. The two majors brought an automatic misconduct penalty and a fine. When this was announced over the public-address system Lindsay leaped from the penalty box to scorch referee Bill Chadwick who accommodated him with a match misconduct for his pains.

"Something wells up inside me," Lindsay said once calmly. "I can't stand somebody trying to show me up."

Fans in out-of-town rinks were inflamed by Lindsay's provocative attitude, his fights with hometown players and, of course, his ability to put the puck in their net. Consequently, few players were ever booed as often or as derisively, a fact that seemed to cause him no particular concern. "As long as the fans don't boo you at home you don't have to worry," he'd say, wearing his crooked grin. "If they boo you on the road you must be doing something to help your club. The other players? I'd like them to be my friends off the ice."

Thus Lindsay, a player who often engaged in battles with Rocket Richard and blistered that volatile player's ears with taunts, trying to unsettle him, had a tremendous off-the-ice respect for the Rocket's talents. "He's a master at pacing himself," he'd say of Richard. "One minute he seems to be skating around aimlessly, and then he gets an opening, strikes, and you're dead. Beautiful."

Thus, too, this terrible-tempered Mr. Bang was a softie around the house between games. His wife Pat said once that he always got up in the middle of the night when their youngsters, Blake and Lynn, were babies crying in the night. "He'd change them and soothe them," she remembered, "and then in the morning he'd bring me orange juice in bed." She was thoughtful a moment. "Of course there was a time I hated him," she said.

That was before they were married when Pat occasionally went to games at the Detroit Olympia. She was a Red Wing supporter but Lindsay's style irritated her. Then they met through a mutual friend. "I discovered, as so many people have, that he's a real Jekyll-Hyde kind of person," she recalled. "I found him delightful."

When Ted and Pat married they moved to Birmingham, a residential suburb of Detroit where their L-shaped gray brick home overlooked the Oakland Hills golf course, had nine rooms and three bathrooms, with a green slate floor and Tennessee ledge-rock fireplace in the recreation room. Such splendor was not part of the Lindsay ménage in Renfrew, Ontario, back on July 29, 1925, when the ninth and, as it turned out, last child was born to Mr. and Mrs. Bert Lindsay. Bert had played hockey in Victoria, British Columbia, and in Renfrew with men like Lester Patrick, Cyclone Taylor, and Newsy Lalonde—immortals in hockey's development. He worked for a trucking firm and when it failed in 1933 he went to Kirkland Lake in far northern Ontario's gold-mining fields, and got a job as manager of the community rink. He moved his six boys and three girls north, including the baby who had been christened Robert Blake Lindsay. The Blake was in honor of a favorite uncle, Blake Johnston, nicknamed Ted, and thus little Robert Blake became Ted, too. Later the boy grew weary of explaining that Ted was a nickname and added Theodore to his list of given names.

He got his first pair of skates when he was nine, given to him by a neighbor, Mrs. Brady; and he wore out the sides of the boots on unsteady ankles almost immediately. Even before he learned to skate he acquired the first in his long list of injuries. He was out one day on an open-air rink in thirty-degree below zero weather with his hands stuffed in his pockets, trying to bring the reluctant skates into line. The severe cold caused a long crack in the ice, which the unsteady boy was unable to avoid. He fell face down, his hands pinned in his pockets, and broke off two front teeth.

Fearing his mother would forbid his skating excursions he didn't mention the broken teeth and adopted a method of smiling, when necessary, without moving his upper lip. But then the teeth became infected and he had to have three of them extracted. Most hockey players wait longer before an inevitable trip to a dentist.

Being a small boy, he learned early to use guile and pugnacity to stay even with the big kids. His teams won a couple of all-Ontario hockey championships, after which he turned down offers from junior clubs in Galt and St. Catharines because they couldn't guarantee he'd be able to keep up his schooling. He entered St. Michael's school in Toronto which iced a strong team in one of Canada's best junior leagues.

Except for an injury, he'd likely have become a member of the Maple Leafs. A fan recommended "a real good kid on St. Mike's" to Leaf coach Hap Day who asked the team's assistant manager, Frank Selke, to take a look at him in action. But Ted had been speared in the calf by a skate point and was hospitalized just then. When Selke, who later became managing director of the Montreal Canadiens, went to watch the St. Michael's team play he saw a winger named Joe Sadler make several clever moves, and he assumed that this was the player in whom Day was interested, and reported to the coach that the boy looked promising. Scouting seems to have been pretty haphazard at the time.

When Lindsay returned to the lineup he was spotted by Carson Cooper, Detroit's chief scout, who followed him for a couple of games during which Lindsay won two fights and scored a goal. That was enough for Cooper and he put Lindsay's name on Detroit's negotiation list.

During the spring, the Oshawa Generals won a berth in the national junior final as champions of eastern Canada. Their coach, the former great rightwinger Charlie Conacher, selected Lindsay as a replacement for an injured player under a rule that permitted such a move, and Ted helped the Generals beat the western Canada champions to win the national championship in 1944. Conacher, who later coached the Chicago Black Hawks, never lost his respect for Lindsay's qualities as a player. He once called him the finest left-winger he'd ever seen. "He's like Ted Williams," Conacher noted. "He can do everything, does it with a flourish, and has a mind of his own."

Lindsay remained a non-conformist from the moment he jumped directly from the juniors to the Red Wings at nineteen until he rejoined Detroit twenty years later after being out of hockey for four years. He devoted those four years to two businesses he'd undertaken during his playing days, a partnership in firms supplying automotive accessories to the automobile industry. He didn't go back to hockey for the money, since business flourished. He went back because he wanted to have his requiem with the Red Wings. By 1964 his old boss Jack Adams had departed the scene to become president of the Central League, and had been replaced by Lindsay's former center, Sid Abel. The third member of that successful line—which was always known as the Production Line, naturally, in Detroit—was Gordie Howe. They'd led the Wings to first-place finishes for four straight years through 1952 and when Abel retired that spring, Lindsay and Howe sparked four more first-place clubs in the next five seasons. Then, after sixteen years, Lindsay, too, called it a career—or thought he had until he heard the fire bells again in 1964.

Though he was thirty-nine then, Lindsay had stayed in condition during his sabbatical by skating regularly and practising with the Red Wings occasionally. He came back the same cantankerous man who'd left, playing all but one game in the seventy-game schedule, picking up twenty-eight scoring points, and adding three more goals in the playoffs against Montreal. He spent 173 minutes glowering in the penalty box, the second-highest number of his career, and took thirty-four more minutes in the playoffs as Chicago slipped past the Red Wings in seven games.

Lindsay came back to the news once more after his second —and final—retirement, and, predictably, he was involved in controversy. He was elected to hockey's Hall of Fame in June 1966 but he declined to attend the Toronto investiture ceremony when he learned that one of the rules excluded the attendance of members' wives and families at a luncheon preceding the induction.

"To hell with that," scowled Terrible Ted. "If my wife and kids can't see the old man honored, what's the point?"

So he stayed in Detroit.

JEAN BELIVEAU

[1931–   ]

Jean beliveau, a bland, bashful, bruising center for the Montreal Canadiens for eighteen seasons, was a unique figure in the history of hockey. He glided serenely through a career in which cities, hockey magnates, and politicians engaged in push-and-pull struggles for his services, and he was virtually a one-man industry paying off the mortgage on a multimillion-dollar rink. He emerged from all this turmoil in the latter stages of his marvellous career to a cool pedestal completely devoid of controversy. Hockey men, who don't concur on much, agree he was one of the most gifted players of all time.

On a mid-summer day in 1971 when Beliveau decided to retire from hockey, he had compiled an awesome record—18 seasons, 1125 games, 507 goals, 712 assists, 1219 points in regular-season play, plus a playoff record of 162 games, 79 goals, 97 assists, and 176 points. He was one of only four players who had scored more than 500 goals—Gordon Howe, Maurice Richard, and Bobby Hull were the others—an achievement made doubly significant by the fact that his hockey life was constantly interrupted by injury. He played a full season only twice in his eighteen years, and missed a total of 234

87

games, the equivalent of three full seventy-eight game schedules.

Nonetheless, when he *was* on the ice, there was no mistaking his proud and regal bearing, a solemn aloofness that set
him apart. There was no mistaking his skills, either. Punch
Imlach, the Buffalo general manager who coached Beliveau
in his amateur days, always regarded him as the finest player
he ever handled, and Conn Smythe, the Toronto founder
who rarely tossed garlands beyond his native city, once ap-
plauded him with three rapid-fire questions: "Where has
there ever been a better stick-handler? Who has ever showed
more savvy? Who ever got a shot away faster?"

Beliveau played his last game of hockey on May 18, 1971,
a Stanley Cup playoff final in which the Canadiens beat Chicago 3–2 at Chicago Stadium to win the world's professional
championship. This 162nd of Beliveau's playoff games left
him two short of the all-time record owned by Red Kelly of
Detroit and Toronto, and it was his tenth Stanley Cup
championship team, a record shared with his teammate
Henri Richard.

The notable lack of argument over Beliveau's place in the
hockey spectrum was one of the more remarkable aspects of
his career, but he wasn't always as clear of controversy. Hot
battles swirled around him before he reached the NHL; in
fact, two prominent hockey executives fought so strenuously
to gain his services as a junior that they seldom again exchanged more than a nod. They were Frank Selke, the managing director of the Canadiens, and Frank Byrne, the owner
of the Quebec Citadels of the Quebec Junior Hockey
League.

To keep Beliveau in Quebec City when he graduated
from junior ranks in 1950, men close to the late Maurice Du-

plessis when he was the powerful premier of Quebec province became involved. It was widely believed in Quebec that the license to operate a tavern in the Montreal Forum —a big money-maker for the Canadian Arena Company which then operated the Canadiens and the Forum—would be revoked if Beliveau were enticed to Montreal by the Canadiens. He stayed in Quebec City for two seasons. Record crowds flocked to worship him and spend money that helped pay for the lavish new Coliseum, a large ice bowl devoid of posts. During Beliveau's first year with the Quebec Aces when they operated in the old Quebec Senior Hockey League, the team drew 281,000 fans in a city of 225,000 people. While during his second, the 1952–53 season, they drew an astonishing 386,334 fans in thirty league games and six playoffs. In the three years after Beliveau left Quebec City and joined the Canadiens, the Aces drew 255,000 the first year, 103,000 the second, and barely 90,000 the third.

"As long as we had Beliveau people knew they were watching the best in the world," said Punch Imlach, who was coach and general manager of the senior Aces in that period, purportedly an amateur team. "They refused to settle for less when he left."

Beliveau delivered on the ice throughout his career. He led the scorers in every league in which he ever played including, of course, the NHL. His rookie year in a game against Boston he scored four goals, and Terry Sawchuk, the Bruin netminder that season, admitted he was beaten cleanly on all of them, a rare confession by any goaltender.

Beliveau was an arresting figure on and off the ice. He stood six-feet-three inches and, by dieting carefully, he kept his weight at 205. He had handsome, sharply defined features, with crisp light brown hair and a warm infrequent smile that illuminated his entire countenance. He viewed the furor that always settled around him in a detached, occasionally self-conscious manner, explaining that in Quebec City the people made a fuss over all the hockey players, and that in Montreal—well, in Montreal everybody always felt a great pride in the Canadiens, eh? Quebec City merchants gave him suits and dinners and even an automobile, and in Montreal he received unprecedented terms for a rookie— $20,000 a year on a five-year contract. This, with a year-round public-relations job with Molson's Brewery at $10,000 a year, plus the hockey bonuses he earned, gave him a yearly income of some $40,000 in the early 1950s. When he became an established professional his income moved onward and upward across the $100,000-a-year level.

With all of this Beliveau remained a remarkably unaffected and actually modest man. "I think the fans overdo it too much," he said once, solemnly and in his deep-throated accented English. "It helps, you know, to be on a good team."

True, the Canadiens were a good team before Beliveau joined them, but they became a great one after. Many old-time fans believed the 1967–68 team, which won the Stanley Cup with the loss of only one game against Boston, Chicago, and St. Louis, was the finest ever. As it happened, this was one of Beliveau's great years, and it was he who dominated all four of the games with the rejuvenated and oncoming Bruins, a team some thought was ripe to derail the Canadiens. Again, he was the incontestable leader in the Chicago triumph, and St. Louis, being new to the NHL and in the expansion West Division, didn't present too severe an obstacle. It was a further measure of Beliveau's contribution that his linemates over the years, some of them veterans from other clubs, had their best seasons when they were playing on the wing beside Beliveau. These included such stars as Yvan Cournoyer, Gilles Tremblay, Dick Duff, Bernie Geoffrion, and Bert Olmstead.

Even as a junior with the Quebec Citadels Beliveau left his mark. His right-wing partner, Rainor Makila, was the second highest scorer on the club (second, of course, to Beliveau) in Jean's final year in junior ranks. The following season Makila didn't even make the Citadel team. Another time, a leftwinger named Claude Larochelle played beside Beliveau for two games when the regular left wing was hurt. Larochelle scored only six goals all season, but he got four of them in the two games beside Beliveau.

Beliveau was so smooth that newcomers to the sport had to watch him for several games before starting to appreciate his finesse. On first glance, because of his size partly, he did not appear to be a particularly fast skater. He had a long fluid stride that was misleading, and he'd get his shot away with a smoothness of motion and speed that fooled the casual observer. In Toronto one night he let go a shot as he cruised across the blueline. Nobody was obstructing the view of the goaltender, Johnny Bower, so the fans were surprised in effete Maple Leaf Gardens to see the puck bulge the back of the net. A few of the more disenchanted booed Bower.

"If I were to compare this guy and Hull I'd say that Hull is far more spectacular but this guy stuns you," growled Bower later. "He shot another one after that goal, and it was even harder. It missed the net, but I heard it whack the boards behind me while I was still moving for it."

Toronto's star rightwinger of the 1930s, Charlie Conacher, was generally conceded to have owned the hardest shot in hockey, at least until Bobby Hull came along with his slapshot, but Conacher himself once said he figured Beliveau's shot was as hard. *"Le Gros Bill,"* grinned Conacher, tackling Beliveau's French nickname, "gets his shot away a little faster, too." The nickname was hung on Beliveau in 1950 by Quebec newspaperman Roland Sabourin. It's part of the title of an old French-Canadian folk song, *Le Voila Le Gros Bill* (Here Comes Big Bill).

To the sorrow of Punch Imlach, who moved into the Toronto hot seat as coach and general manager for a decade in 1957, it was he who developed the speed of Beliveau's shot and his skating stride. These events came about when the two of them were allied in Quebec City. Imlach noticed that Beliveau was missing occasional scoring chances because he was about a half-stride slow in getting into position. So, in practice sessions, Imlach placed a player in the center of the faceoff circle at one end of the ice, and lined Beliveau behind him on the circumference of the circle. Then Imlach dropped the puck onto the player's stick in the center of the circle, and Beliveau's job was to overtake him as he sped up the ice.

"At first he couldn't catch his man," Imlach related years later, bemoaning a classic Beliveau performance that had helped sink Imlach's Buffalo Sabres, "but after a couple of weeks he could." Then Imlach ingeniously assigned a fresh player to the circle each time he dropped the puck. Soon he was overtaking the fifteenth man nearly as fast as the first.

For shooting drills it wasn't unusual for Beliveau to line up twenty pucks on the blueline after a team practice and bang away at them for an hour; he even developed control of a slapshot in his diligence. Newsmen scoffed when Imlach made this claim, and he responded by dumping a pail of pucks on the ice. "Where do you want him to put 'em?" he asked blandly.

A spot was indicated just under the crossbar of the goal. Beliveau skated toward a puck, brought back his stick, and followed through on a spanking slapshot. The puck ticked the crossbar at the point indicated, and ricocheted into the net.

"He doesn't really slap it," Imlach elucidated later. "He cocks his wrists like a golfer and strokes it."

No one was ever quite sure how Beliveau became so good so early. He inherited neither his size nor his dedication to hockey from his family. His father, Arthur Beliveau, had no interest in athletics and no size for them; and his mother, the former Laurette Dubé, was equally dispassionate about sports. Jean, born August 31, 1931, in Three Rivers, Quebec, was the first of five sons and two daughters. A third daughter was struck by a car and died in hospital when she was five in 1946.

Beliveau began attracting attention when he was sixteen. By then *la famille* Beliveau had moved from Three Rivers to another Quebec town, Victoriaville, a hundred miles east of Montreal where Arthur Beliveau worked as a foreman with a water and power company. There was no junior hockey there but Jean hung around the rink after school and played with any team that needed an extra man. One evening Frank Byrne, owner of the Quebec Citadels juniors, got a telephone call from Lucien Duchene, a former Citadel goaltender then playing for the Victoriaville seniors. "I want you to come right down," Duchene told Byrne. "There's a kid here, fifteen or sixteen, who practiced with us today and he damn near knocked my head off with a shot. He's only a kid but he's big and he's all bone."

About the same time, Montreal's Frank Selke had become interested in Beliveau when the coach of the Victoriaville team, Rollie Hebert, recommended him. Selke, a wise little man who'd toiled for years in Toronto as Conn Smythe's assistant before moving to Montreal to become boss of the Canadiens, made the trip, and tried to sign the strapping youngster the moment he saw him make a few moves on the ice. But Selke couldn't make much headway with the Beliveau family because none of them spoke English. So he made a succeeding trip with Montreal defenseman Butch Bouchard as his interpreter. Not the most rewarding one, as it turned out.

"Arthur Beliveau advised Butch that hockey players are bums," Selke recalled, a sentiment apparently based on the fact Arthur Beliveau believed his son was wasting too much time at the rink, to the detriment of his studies.

But Frank Byrne had more success with the senior Beliveau, pointing out that he'd make certain Jean lived with a fine family in Quebec City, be paid a good salary, and go to school. This seemed to change the mind of Beliveau *père;* a salary of $7500 for his sixteen-year-old son presumably also helped him withdraw his objection. Meantime Selke, recognizing that he'd lost the battle, took steps to win the war; he put Jean's name on a Canadien negotiation list, thereby preventing other NHL teams from trying to corral professional rights.

Two years later the Canadiens made another move on Beliveau, but powerful political forces in Quebec City, the provincial capital, wanted him to remain in the old historic city to play with the senior Aces (and help pay for the new Coliseum). Numerous hockey figures in Quebec at the time claimed it to be common knowledge that the Forum management in Montreal had been advised that if the Canadiens outbid the Aces for Beliveau the Forum's tavern license would be cancelled. Once, when this point was mentioned to

Selke, he responded indirectly.

"I have no criticism of the peculiar methods adopted by the Quebec people to keep Beliveau down there," he said. "I don't play politics. . . . If there is anything phony going on, you can't pin it on the Quebec premier Maurice Duplessis. He told me to do what I thought was best for sport in Quebec and not to worry about political pressure."

So perhaps Selke decided that what was best for sport in Quebec was to keep the Forum tavern open. In any event, Beliveau stayed in Quebec City, playing amateur for $20,000 during the twenty-week hockey season, and got an additional $2500 as a public relations representative for a dairy (you never outgrow your need for milk). Indeed, *Le Gros Bill* might have played out his career in Quebec City—or at least until the mortgage was lifted on the rink—but after two years Quebec's Senior Hockey League voted to become a recognized professional league. The instant that happened Beliveau became the property of the Canadiens because of Selke's foresight in having nailed down his professional services. Quebec City had lost whatever hammerlock it had on the young man through political pressure; for once the Quebec league took on professional status there was nothing to prevent, say, the New York Rangers from drafting Beliveau. Thus it became clear to all that if Beliveau were to be retained at least by the province, the Canadiens would have to take him. So in the summer of 1953 Montreal signed him to a five-year contract.

At that time the NHL had what it called the "three-game trial" rule, which meant that a well-paid amateur was permitted to play with the pros for three games a season without forfeiting his so-called amateur standing. Yet even while he was performing for Quebec City, Beliveau was making occasional forays into a Canadien uniform. In 1950–51 he played two games, getting a goal and an assist, and two seasons later he played three games. He scored three goals in one of them against Chuck Rayner of the Rangers, showing that even then he was thoroughly ready for the NHL. Two years later, in the spring of 1954, he became a full-fledged Canadien and scored two goals and had three assists in an 8–1 shellacking of Boston. The next year he was hammering poor Terry Sawchuk in the Bruin net for four goals—three of them power-play efforts within a span of forty-four seconds. In 1956 he scored the first goal of a 3–1 Montreal victory over Detroit which gave the Canadiens the Stanley Cup, his first of ten with the Montrealers. The goal was his twelfth of the playoffs which tied a record long owned by Maurice Richard and one that stood until Boston's Phil Esposito got thirteen goals in the 1970 playoffs.

And so it went all through his career. When Jean wasn't tying records he was breaking them, moving in tall icy serenity above the madding crowd—or so it seemed. His final year, the 1970–71 season, was one of his most memorable. Even the prime minister of the country, Pierre Elliott Trudeau, had public applause for him. This came on March 24, Jean Beliveau Night at the Montreal Forum, when instead of modestly accepting the largesse that accrues at these functions Beliveau requested that a fund be organized whose donations would go to underprivileged children across Canada. "Rarely has the career of an athlete been so exemplary," said the prime minister. "By his courage, his sense of discipline and honor, his lively intelligence and finesse, by his magnificent team spirit, Beliveau has given new prestige to hockey."

He gave it even more a few weeks later when the Canadiens engaged the Bruins in the first round of the Stanley

Cup playoffs. This was the celebrated series in which the Bruins, coming off the most remarkable record-breaking orgy in NHL history, were expected to destroy the record book in the playoffs, as well. Boston goaltender Gerry Cheevers made an immortal observation at the time. "The Flying Frenchmen," he remarked, civilly, "go slightly glassy-eyed when they get thinking of their tradition and their pride and all that bullshit." Beaten 3–1 in the first game and trailing 5–1 in the second, the Canadiens suddenly went slightly glassy-eyed. Beliveau, who hadn't done much for five periods, scored two goals within ninety seconds and assisted on a third. When the score got tied at 5–5 Beliveau went behind the Boston cage, shoved Bruins aside as though he were a pinboy clearing the gutter, outmuscled everyone he could reach, and got the puck out to John Ferguson in front for the goal that proved the winner in an electrifying 7–5 Montreal victory. And Jean's four points moved him to the top of the all-time list of playoff scorers.

Two weeks later, the Bruins brushed aside, *Le Gros Bill* got three assists in a 6–1 Montreal victory over Minnesota in the next Stanley Cup round, and this gave him the record for most assists in the playoffs. And a couple of weeks after *that,* with Minnesota disposed of, he went to work on Chicago. On May 11 he scored his 79th playoff goal, second in history only to Rocket Richard's eighty-two, and five nights later he collected two more assists for a career total of ninety-seven in the playoffs, six more than runner-up Gordie Howe.

Small wonder then, with the Stanley Cup in the bag once more, he announced his retirement on June 9. There was nothing left to shoot at.

GORDIE HOWE

[1928–   ]

W HEN GORDIE HOWE retired from the NHL in September 1971 it was not an easy thing to get a meaningful perspective on his career; every cold hard fact tended to be a superlative and many of the cold hard facts were unique and seemed likely to stay that way. He simply outdistanced everybody by so wide a margin that even the diminution in the quality of the game that followed expansion in 1967 appeared unlikely to bring his records within anyone's reach for years and years. For instance, for a player just beginning a career in the NHL it would be necessary for him to average 100 points a season for eighteen years to catch him, or if he set his sights on Howe's goal total he'd have to average better than fifty-two goals a season for fifteen years. Thus, a recital of Howe's achievements during his long career blurs toward meaninglessness. However . . .

● Howe played twenty-five full seasons for one team, the Detroit Red Wings (only one other player, Allan Stanley of New York, Chicago, Boston, Toronto, and Philadelphia, played more than twenty).

● Howe played 1687 league games (only one other player, Alex Delvecchio, also of Detroit, played more than 1500).

● Howe scored 786 goals (only one other player, Bobby Hull of Chicago, scored more than 600, and only two others, Maurice Richard and Jean Beliveau of Montreal, scored more than 500).

● Howe had 1023 assists (only Delvecchio and Beliveau had more than 700).

● Howe had 1809 points (only Beliveau and Delvecchio had more than 1200).

● Howe scored twenty or more goals through twenty-two *consecutive* seasons (second best was Maurice Richard who had fourteen consecutive twenty-goal seasons).

Some people enjoy a profitable career simply by surviving twelve seasons in the NHL. Howe was picked on the No. 1 All-Star team twelve times. He was picked on the No. 2 team nine times. In fact, in twenty-two consecutive seasons he missed one or the other of the All-Star teams only once. That was the 1954–55 season when he was fifth on the scoring list and had a pretty good year by ordinary standards. However, it was also the year that two other rightwingers had remarkable years, Richard and his teammate Bernie (Boom Boom) Geoffrion. Geoffrion led the league in scoring, one point ahead of Richard, and neither could be kept off the All-Star lineup. Poor old Howe had to settle for a Stanley Cup triumph by his Detroit teammates who shaded—who else? —Richard and Geoffrion and the rest of the Canadiens in the Cup final. Howe scored three goals in one of the games to pace a 5–1 victory, and then he scored the winner in the seventh and deciding game. Even in the year of his eclipse, as it were, he dominated.

And there were other little odds and ends. He won the Hart Trophy as the league's most valuable player six times, twice more than celebrated Eddie Shore, the old Boston defenseman. In a twenty-three year stretch, he played in the All-Star game twenty-two times, with an unequalled record of fourteen straight appearances. He scored 188 game-winning goals, he scored thirty or more goals in fourteen seasons, he was in the Stanley Cup playoffs nineteen times, and so on and so on until the mind begins to boggle.

Sometimes during the latter stages of Howe's astonishing run it seemed he had been around forever. For instance as the decade of the 1970s began, New York's Brad Park, Boston's Bobby Orr, and Montreal's Ken Dryden had become household words in hockey, but none had even been born the year Howe played his first full NHL season. Boston's Phil Esposito was an eight-year veteran the year Howe hung up his tack; he was four the year Gordie broke in. Or, on a different level, the year Howe entered the NHL Joe Louis retained the heavyweight boxing championship by knocking out Billy Conn in the thirteenth round in Yankee Stadium. Bob Feller was the winning pitcher in the All-Star game, Hank Greenberg hit forty-four home runs to lead both leagues, and the base-stealing leader was Pete Reiser of the Brooklyn Dodgers. And who won the U.S. Open? Not Arnie or Jack; they'd never been heard of. No, it was Lloyd Mangrum, who beat Vic Ghezzi and Byron Nelson in a playoff.

Through all those years from the mid-1940s and through the 1950s and the 1960s, there was always Gordie Howe putting the biscuit in the basket. For nineteen consecutive years in that period he was among the league's top *five* scorers, and in six of them he was the scoring champion, responding to the tumult with all the exuberant zest of a man boarding a crowded bus at rush hour. While his teammates jubilantly thumped his back and the crowd roared its endless ecstacy he'd hang his head solemnly, even *shyly,* and skate in short, weary strides to the Detroit bench after every goal. There, he'd sit with his arms crossed, his elbows pressed against his thighs, and stare impassively at the scarred floor until the hubbub subsided, blinking furiously with a kind of nervous twitch that developed later in his career and brought him the nickname Blinky.

For all his heroics, Howe was as colorless as a piece of tape. He had none of the flair of Rocket Richard or Bobby Hull; he was, visually, an honest workman, no more. People who watched him play only occasionally wondered what the fuss was about. He had marvellous reflexes and great anticipation, and these took the style from his performance, giving him goals with an unseen flick, presenting him with position that often seem fortuitous. He was a Joe DiMaggio among hockey players, always in the right place at the right time, never seeming to sweat for anything. He was born fifth in a family of nine on the wheat-growing prairies of Saskatchewan, and he looked it—not fifth; a farmer. As a boy he sought to overcome a lack of minerals in his infancy, which had left him with a weak spine, by working for a construction company, mixing cement, and by hanging from door frames and swinging his hips hour after hour. Consequently he had a thick upper body, large sloping shoulders, big arms, and strong wrists. "He reminds me of one of those legendary Texans," his old boss, Jack Adams, used to say, beaming as he peered at Howe in the Detroit dressing room. "His actions do his talking. I keep waiting for him to say 'Yup'."

He looked relaxed and low-keyed and he never did talk much, but perhaps the eye twitch was a giveaway of inner tensions he never showed, and he deliberately set about imposing distractions upon himself as soon as a game ended. If the Wings were on the road he'd organize a bridge game the moment the players settled on an airplane for the return home. It relieved the post-game letdown. And after games at the Detroit Olympia he'd join his wife Colleen in the lobby and then drive to a quiet restaurant en route to their home in Lathrup, a residential suburb twenty miles northwest of downtown. Later the same evening he'd stretch out on a couch and watch an hour or so of television, forgetting hockey completely in an untaxing late late show, before mooching quietly to bed.

From the street in Lathrup the Howe home looked like any other ranch-style bungalow, but it turned out to be a tri-level affair with a second floor built into a gentle slope at the back. He'd spend most of his off-season poking around this place, pulling weeds, cutting the grass, dabbing here and there with a paint brush. The house was built of red brick and white frame with four bedrooms and four baths to accommodate the six Howes. Marty, the oldest boy, was born in 1954, followed by Mark in 1955, Cathy in 1959, and Murray in 1960.

When Gordie padded around this house—usually in bare feet, a faded T-shirt, and crude-fitting shorts flapping at the knees—he presented a picture difficult to reconcile with his hockey image: tough, rugged, tireless, versatile, and especially no man to mess with, all elbows, stick, and fists when he needed them. Before he was through he ran his penalty total to 1643 minutes (plus another 218 in playoffs) and since this represented more than thirty-one full games in the penalty box—his was hardly a tranquil personality. Still, on the testimony of Colleen, a serene though determined person with pastel coloring, there would be no more relaxed a man around the house than the padding figure in the crazy pants. Their relationship appeared to be warm and unruffled and unaffected. "We met in a bowling alley," Colleen recalled one afternoon in the kitchen while preparing lunch. "A boy I knew introduced us. Gordie was a noted player with the Red Wings then but his name meant nothing to me; I didn't follow hockey. But after we'd bowled awhile I liked his quiet way, and I began to follow hockey after that." She was soft-spoken that afternoon, eyes light blue and solemn, hair shoulder-length and light in its coloring. "He's a very thoughtful father, and patient too," she said of her husband, "but he's stern when it's necessary—you know, with discipline."

She led the way to the activities room, as she called a broad expanse in the cellar. "Gordie seems to be able to do well at anything he tries," she said, indicating row upon row of shelves. "He made those, and he put in a whole kitchen for his mother in Saskatoon. Anything he does, he does wholeheartedly."

Jack Adams used to make this point, too; he'd say Howe could excel at anything, that he could have been a star at several sports. "He has the build and temperament for professional sports but, more than that, he's a student," Adams once said. "He shoots golf in the low seventies, he's an excellent ten-pin bowler, and he could have played big-league baseball. He occasionally works out with the Tigers, you know. One year, before he settled here, he went home to Saskatoon and hit .375 in a pretty good semi-pro league they had going out there."

Through all of his twenty-five years in the NHL Howe

103

spent far more time on the ice than most players. Apart from his regular shift, he went out when Detroit was shorthanded to kill penalties and naturally he was the kingpin of the Red Wing power play. And in the late stages of close games, he was usually sent on the ice out of turn, either to help protect a slim lead or try to overcome a deficit. Once, after Sid Abel had succeeded Adams as coach, he was asked if Howe ever complained about overwork. Boot, as Abel was called, nearly dropped out from under his hat.

"Complain? Blink? Are you kidding?" he said. "When he comes off and he's been sitting on the bench a minute or so, he turns to me and says, 'I'm ready, Boot.' And after another thirty seconds, if things are tight, he'll turn again and say, 'You sore at me, Boot?' Blink doesn't go much for sitting."

Howe never felt he was overworked. "When I'm feeling good I figure I'm not out enough," he said once when the matter came up. He always had a laconic way of speaking. Somebody once noted that he seemed to score a lot of goals by setting up in front of the net looking for rebounds and passouts. "You don't score much from behind," he said. Another time he was playing a golf exhibition near Toronto with three of Canada's best pros, George Knudson, Al Balding, and Stan Leonard. He admitted he was far more nervous with 200 people watching than in any Stanley Cup final. He was asked why it mattered when he wasn't expected to excel. He hesitated, then offered tentatively: "Pride in not making a fool of yourself?" Then somebody wondered if he knew the source of the determination he'd shown through his long career. Again he answered with a question. "Shyness, maybe, eh?"

Even at forty Howe was often the first man on the ice in practices and the last to leave. Several years ago when he,

Boot Abel, and Ted Lindsay were making beautiful music for the Wings, they'd stay out for at least half an hour after practice sessions to work on passing and their own maneuvers. Then Howe would put in another thirty minutes firing pucks at the net where Abel was stationed, guiding deflections through the posts.

"There are always things you can sharpen," he was saying even after his twenty-second season, a remarkable one for anybody and astonishing for an old guy of forty. He scored thirty-nine goals, his highest output in eleven seasons, was the league's third highest point-scorer with eighty-two, and was picked—of course, of course—on the No. 1 All-Star team. "Like, when you're shifting to fool a guy, you tend to shift away from his stick-side, right? I mean, the stick-side is his best side and he can hit you better on that side. But he sees this, he knows where you're gonna make your move, which way you're gonna go. So you've got to go the other way now and then, and you can forget this if you're playing from reflex." That was a long speech for Howe, but he was always patient with slow learners.

On the bench he studied goaltenders, and obviously expansion gave him a lot of these to study. When Howe broke in, he had five goaltenders to worry about; while in the first year of expansion there were twenty-eight on Detroit's eleven-team list of rivals, a fairly graphic illustration of the dilution that expansion brought to big-league hockey, since it cast twenty-odd netmen onto the NHL scene who hadn't been good enough to labor there before. At any rate, what Howe studied, sitting there on the Detroit bench, were the reflexive actions of these strangers so that when he was on the ice he'd know what to do to beat them. Howe, by the way, reaped a pretty fair harvest on the watered-down product; he scored 137 goals in four seasons, an average of just over thirty-four a year, compared with his output of not quite thirty-one a season in the old six-team league. To some, that spread wasn't too startling, but perhaps they forgot that Howe was forty, forty-one, forty-two, and forty-three years of age during his four-year fling in lotusland.

But, of course, he was studying goaltenders long before expansion, searching out their habits. "You don't usually have much time to look, the way those big bears come belting," he said of defensemen protecting their netminder by hoisting people out of the goal area, "so when you get the puck you've got to let her go real quick. So, if you know a guy goes down a lot, say, you put her high."

One who caused him a good deal of trouble over the years was Johnny Bower when he was with the Rangers and, later, the Leafs. But then, studying him carefully, Howe spotted a flaw.

"Old John leans," he revealed, "so I just waited whenever I had a break on him until he leaned, and then I'd put the puck into the opposite side. I got a breakaway in the playoffs against him one time. I waited, he leaned, and I drilled the puck away from him. Would you believe it, the puck hit the handle of his stick." The score was 4–4 when that happened in sudden-death overtime. Howe's carefully researched shot should have won the game. As it turned out, Toronto eventually got the fifth goal.

Howe, scoring as often as he did, was nonetheless the compleat team player, a point Jack Adams was fond of making, usually going back to the spring of 1952 to illustrate. That year, Howe had a shot at Rocket Richard's then record of fifty goals for the season.

"He had around forty-four or forty-five, with maybe five

games to go," Adams reconstructed. "I told Tommy Ivan, who was coaching our club at the time, to put Gordie out there every chance he got. We had the Howe–Abel–Lindsay line then, but instead of going for goals Gordie kept passing the puck off to Sid. I couldn't figure it out, and then Tommy tipped me. 'He knows Boot gets a bonus for twenty goals, Jack. He's trying to set *Boot* up.' "

As it turned out, neither made it. Howe got forty-six goals that year, and Abel settled for seventeen. The following season Howe almost caught Rocket's record; he got forty-nine goals, a career high.

Though Howe was laconic, he was never uncommunicative. Indeed, in a few graphic words, he often said it all. There were reports, for instance, that he was emotionally distressed when his chum Lindsay was traded to Chicago by Adams. He was asked if he were indeed dismayed by what many construed as management's callousness.

"News to me," he said matter-of-factly.

Well, had he then reconciled himself to the fact *he* might be traded?

"That's how I got *my* chance."

He never was a talker, which is probably why he didn't wind up playing for the New York Rangers. As a gangling boy of fourteen he attended a Ranger camp in Winnipeg, but Lester Patrick, the New York coach and general manager at the time, apparently was not struck by him. Lester kept asking him if he were related to "the other Howe." This was Syd Howe, a star of the era with Ottawa, St. Louis, and later Detroit. Gordie kept telling him, "Nope."

He went home to Saskatoon after a week and played juvenile hockey, impressing Fred Pinkney, a Detroit scout, who sent him to Windsor, Ontario, the following fall to the Wing training camp. Detroit liked him as a prospect and tried to assign him to their junior farm team in Galt but the Canadian Amateur Hockey Association refused to sanction his transfer from Saskatchewan to Ontario. Rather than let him escape, Detroit kept him out of hockey for a year, using him only in practices. The fall of 1945, though, he did so well at training camp that Jack Adams decided to turn him professional, even at seventeen. He was assigned to Tommy Ivan at Omaha, a big, solemn, scared shy kid. And he *was* shy. Of his year in the United States Hockey League he later remembered that the lights of Dallas, in particular, awed him. "I used to go by all the real nice-looking eating places to eat in the drug store," he remembered. "I just couldn't get myself to go into those nice places."

But he had that innate determination to improve and there was nothing shy about him on the ice. One night, playing in St. Louis, he became involved in a fierce fracas with Myles Lane, a former NHLer and a very rugged defenseman. The exchange developed rapidly when Lane knocked Howe down with a right-hand wallop. Howe scrambled to his feet and Lane knocked him down again. Once more Howe got up and this time he tore past Lane's punches and gave the big defenseman a going-over. That night, Tommy Ivan phoned Adams in Detroit. "Jack, we've got something here," he said. "This big skinny kid, Howe, has all the guts he needs and he hits like a pile-driver."

Thus, when Howe was eighteen, he was ripe for the NHL. To that point he'd been fairly free of injury, despite a rupture operation after his season in Omaha. But early in his first year with Detroit he was checking New York's Bryan Hextall (two decades later he was checking Hextall's *sons,* Bryan of the Pittsburgh Penguins and Dennis of the Minnesota North Stars) and then he felt his left knee cave. Later he required surgery for cartilage removal. He seemed headed for big things the following season until Pat Egan, a Ranger defenseman, crashed him into the boards, tearing cartilage in his other knee, bringing on another operation at Christmas. He was back, amazingly, in a month, and then out again with a shoulder separation. But he came back from that to shine in the playoffs, leading all pointgetters with eight goals and three assists. By then he was on his way.

Off the ice, he strove to improve, too. He shuddered when a Detroit brewery invited him to represent the firm at luncheons and functions at which he showed hockey movies and answered questions from the floor. The idea of standing on his feet and talking to people made him sweat but he drove himself to do it. "I used to come home soaked and mentally beat," he recalled once. Aware that his vocabulary was limited (he left school in the ninth grade) he worked on crossword puzzles, books, and magazines to improve it. After a few years he grew relatively at ease in public, and in later years became a wry and observant hockey analyst on national television those years the Wings were eliminated.

In 1958 he participated in one of the most unforgettable of all hockey fights, one that became part of the Howe legend. The party of the second part was the Ranger defenseman Lou Fontinato, the New York policeman, a tough and tempestuous fellow. They clashed near the Ranger net, and immediately began swinging. In no time, it seemed, the ice was running red with Fontinato's blood, his nose flattened by Howe's fierce pummeling. Phil Watson, the New York coach, later remarked that Howe's punches had the effect of so jarring his club that it knocked them right out of the playoffs. They had needed only a tie in any one of their final five games to cinch a playoff spot. But they didn't get the tie and Toronto, winning its last six games in a row, sneaked past them by a single point. "We never recovered from Louie's pasting," Watson said. "His nose looked like the subway'd hit it."

It's a fact that the Howe saga almost never happened. In 1950 his career very nearly came to an end, and so did his life. In an incredibly vicious series with Toronto, Howe raced across the ice to check Ted Kennedy near the end of the first playoff game. Kennedy, cruising near the boards, pulled up short as Howe slammed toward him and Howe crashed headlong into the boards. He crumpled to the ice, blood streaming from his nose and eye.

A brain specialist ordered an immediate operation to remove fluid causing pressure on the brain. Twenty-four hours later, headlines in the three Detroit newspapers shouted that his life hung suspended.

The incident added animosity to the riotous hockey series, and seemed to incite Detroit's determination to win, which they did in seven games. Then, with the fast-recovering Howe able to leave the hospital ten days later, they won the Stanley Cup by beating the Rangers in the final. Howe, his head heavily bandaged, joined his team on the ice after the game when the delirious Detroit fans began to chant, "We want Howe!"

For a time the following season the Red Wing management insisted Howe wear a helmet to protect a small hole that had been drilled over his right ear during the operation. He wore it for a time, then discarded it.

"Makes me sweat," Gordie Howe explained in that way of his.

PHIL ESPOSITO

[1942–   ]

$\mathcal{P}$HIL ESPOSITO, a large, rich hockey player with chronically sore feet, was discovered in 1969 during the sixth year of his NHL career and became a superstar in September 1972 at the Lenin Sports Palace in far-off Moscow.

For nine years he languished, more or less, in the shadows of Bobby Hull, his teammate for four years on the Chicago Black Hawks, and Bobby Orr, with whom he frolicked for the next five on the Boston Bruins. He did things in that period that had never been done before, but the combination of accomplishing them on the same ice floe as Hull or Orr, and doing them in a gangling, almost awkward manner contrived to keep him on the shady side of the street.

"I'm the first to admit that I don't electrify a crowd," Phil once said. "I just don't have the charisma. I just plod along, nice and slow, though I get my goals."

He did, indeed, in those tumultuous nine years, and he brought the crowds to their feet a few times in that period, too. In 1969, the year he became something more than Bobby Hull's center or Bobby's Orr's teammate to the public, he scored a hundred points for the first time in history. He did it on the March 1 weekend that year. He got his ninety-eighth point, the one that broke the existing record shared by Hull and Stan Mikita, against the New York Rangers on a Saturday night in Boston, and the next night against Pittsburgh he hit the unprecedented century. Both times the packed and smoky old Boston Garden erupted. On Sunday, 200 men's hats were swept from the ice by impassive attendants wearing rubbers and shoving scrapers, and the crowds' teeming emotion for Espo's high moment was also illustrated by a flash of pink in the pile of debris—a brassiere. He became a record-breaker of gargantuan proportion before the season was out, piling in 126 points. That total broke the old Hull–Mikita mark by twenty-eight, and his seventy-seven assists fractured Mikita's old standard by fifteen.

Two seasons later his feats were even more unlikely. He got a scarcely credible 152 points, made up of seventy-six goals—another record by farther than a strong boy can throw a big red apple, as Canadian syndicated sports columnist Jim Coleman phrased it—and seventy-six assists. And the year after *that* he cooled off to a mere sixty-six goals and sixty-seven assists, either of which represented a pretty good season's total output for most players.

Still, there was a reluctance to enshrine Espo. Nit-pickers noted that he was toiling among the dregs of expansion, that he was picking up a lot of Bobby Orr's garbage, banging in rebounds after Orr had mesmerized everybody, that nobody who skated like *that* could possibly share a podium with the all-time greats. He didn't have Rocket Richard's flair, Gordie Howe's versatility, Bobby Hull's shot, Jean Beliveau's cool elegance, or Bobby Orr's leadership. All he had was this skill in front of the goal, a sort of magic wand that somehow got the puck into the net, and a four-year contract for

$600,000 (if his critics had thought of it, they could have applauded his *lawyer* for that).

But then through unexpected circumstances Phil Esposito finally emerged as a superstar in the autumn of 1972 when Canada met Russia in the greatest hockey series in the history of the game, eight magnificent confrontations that turned all of Canada inside out (3,000 Canadians flew to Moscow for the final four games there and, at home, more than 16 million viewers tuned into television—compared with 7.8 million for the Stanley Cup playoffs the previous spring and 12 million who watched the moon landing—in a country with some 22 million population). And in that series Esposito revealed that each of his parts was as great as the whole. With flair, leadership, versatility, and a wondrous defiance, he was the inspiration for a stunning comeback in which Canada won three games in a row in a Russian arena that was absolutely alive with tension, excitement, and drama to beat the pattern-passing, superbly drilled Russian national team four games to three, with one tie. And he did it all without Bobby Orr and without Bobby Hull, neither of whom could play.

The series was designed as a test between the best players of the two countries but it didn't turn out that way because the NHL worked from a position of authority to ban any players not signed to 1972–73 contracts. This, of course, excluded those who had jumped to the World Hockey Association, including the instant millionaire Bobby Hull. Orr was out because of knee surgery following Boston's Stanley Cup victory in the spring. He was with the team as a sort of celebrity cheerleader during the first four games in Montreal, Toronto, Winnipeg, and Vancouver, and he went to Moscow for the final four games. But his knee didn't respond, although he tried it repeatedly at practice sessions. His emotional involvement was so intense that he found it impossible to go to the rink for the final game. He watched it on television in his room at the Intourist Hotel, miles from the wildly raucous Lenin arena.

Esposito's take-charge propensities began to emerge for all to see in Game 4 when a Vancouver throng of some 16,000 turned on the Canadians as Russia jumped ahead 2–0 and eventually won the game 5–3. The fans responded as though they were being hoodwinked by Team Canada, whom most everyone had picked to win the series in eight straight. But when the Russians turned out to be far more skilled than most people had dreamed, when it appeared that they had overtaken the skills of the players from the land that had nurtured the. game, one of the few areas in which Canada presumed to hold world supremacy, the fans turned on the players who were letting *them* down. On national television after the game Esposito told the millions watching how disheartened the players were at the way they'd been ridiculed, that they were doing the best they could under less than ideal conditions, that the Russians deserved full credit for their skills. He said it with passion and even anger.

When the team went to Stockholm to accustom itself to the wider European ice surfaces, Esposito was the kingpin in a 4–1 win and a 4–4 tie against the Swedish national team. Ranting and raving as two European referees made mincemeat of the rules, waving derisively at the hostile crowds, Espo was the dominant figure, never an elegant one but a dynamic force, popping in crucial goals (such as the tying one in the final minute of the second game) standing in the penalty box to exhort his teammates or leading the forays on the ice, chasing the Swedish coach in the runway between

114

the dressing rooms after that coach had shouted an insult from the bench.

By Moscow, he was the unquestioned leader. In the four games there he killed penalties, worked the power plays, took his regular shift, fought anybody who got in his way, waved belligerently at the crowd when they whistled their displeasure, and did all of this in an atmosphere that would have given pause to a lesser man. For one thing, the rink was alive with armed and uniformed Soviets, hardly a milieu where most people would choose to challenge authority. The fans were subdued, totally restrained, even submissive, throughout the first game in complete contrast to the exuberant Canadian contingent waving cowbells and banners, blowing horns and chanting for goals. As the series wore on, however, the Russians began whistling shrilly to drown out the Canadian cheers and chants, and this created a rising tension throughout the big ice palace, the suggestion of an impending riot. Yet none of this seemed to affect Esposito's relentlessly bellicose style. He might just as well have been engaged in a quiet little tong war at Madison Square Garden, battling the Rangers and infuriating the fans.

That final game a new peak was achieved in the tense chemistry of the huge throng, more than 15,000 jammed into a seating capacity for 13,000, clogging every aisle and standing three deep in the uppermost reaches. The Russians got ahead 5–3 by the end of the second period. They were riding a great crescendo of sound generated by their now completely untethered fans, and appeared to be at the very peak of their game. Canadian writers, gathering as a long-faced little group in a wide rotunda under the seats during intermission, were convinced the Russians had reached a mechanical and emotional plateau that simply could not be turned back.

"I just hope," one of them said, "that we can stay reasonably close. I mean, 8–3 or 9–3 would be a terrible wrap-up."

Enter Esposito. Early in the period he fought off the Russians in front of the net and banged in a goal to make it 5–4. Then he threw a pass to the zipping Yvan Cournoyer of the Canadiens for the tying goal. Suddenly the momentum had swung, but wait! The light back of the net hadn't gone on, and within seconds, half a dozen armed and uniformed Russians in khaki greatcoats and hats were milling around a box seat across the ice from the Canadian bench. They were manhandling Alan Eagleson, the players' association boss. Eagleson, who appeared to grow progressively more paranoid as the series continued and who acquired the epithet *nekulturny,* which translates as yahoo, in Russia, had thrown a tantrum when the light didn't go on. The uniforms were removing him from his seat and taking him God knows where, until Esposito and Pete Mahovlich of the Canadiens leaped off the bench and led a swarm of Canadian players to Eagleson's side. Sticks waving high in the air, they wrested him clear and escorted him, slipping and sliding, back across the ice to their bench. Then, to add to the tumult, two seemingly endless lines of soldiers marched into the arena from an entrance back of the Russian net and completely encircled the ice surface, standing shoulder to shoulder in a wide aisle along the boards. An uneasy peace settled over the sports palace, and for ten minutes of playing time the teams roared up and down the ice. An orange-faced clock behind the Russian goal ticked off the seconds, and now there was less than a minute left. Esposito, tireless and relentless, went to the corner for the puck as Canadian coach Harry Sinden tried to switch his lines. Paul Henderson of Toronto got out at left wing, and he and Cournoyer rushed into the Russian zone. Esposito got the puck across to Henderson from the corner, but a Russian defender tied him up. Esposito rushed over to retain possession of the puck for Canada and the Russian goaltender Tretiak blocked his shot. Henderson ripped free of his check and swiped twice at the puck. The second time, it went in. It was 6–5 for Canada. There were thirty-four seconds on the clock. All Esposito had done in the third period, when it appeared certain that the Russians were coming, was score a goal and get two assists. What more could be asked of a *superstar?*

Yes, recognition was a long time coming. For even as a youngster he had trouble convincing people that he had anything to offer except enthusiasm. As a boy in his native Sault Ste. Marie, called the Soo, where he was born on February 20, 1942, he played for the Algoma Contractors, a bantam team sponsored by Algoma gold mines for whom his father Pat was a foreman. At seventeen he wasn't good enough for Junior A so he went to Sarnia, north of Detroit on Georgian Bay, and played Junior B. He quit high school to concentrate on hockey, earning $27.50 a week in Sarnia. Then he moved up to the St. Catharines Tee Pees in Junior A where he got $57.50 a week plus room and board. During the summers he drove a truck at home in the Soo and banged punctured tennis balls at his goaltending brother Tony, fifteen months his junior, who later went to the Montreal Canadiens and then to the Chicago Black Hawks where he too became a star.

Phil turned pro with Chicago, the sponsor of the St. Catharines juniors, for a $1000 signing bonus and a $3800 salary. The Hawks assigned him to their pro farm club at the Soo shortly before the franchise was shifted to St. Louis in the Central league. He got ninety points in seventy-one

117

games, including thirty-five goals, and his reward was a $5500 salary for his second season. He had eighty points in forty-three games when the Hawks brought him up to the NHL, and he spent most of the balance of the season sitting on their bench. The Hawk general manager put him on a two-year contract then, at $10,500 for the first and $12,500 for the second. He got twenty-three goals and thirty-two assists in that first year, playing center with Bobby Hull and Chico Maki, and added twenty-seven goals and twenty-six assists in his second. That brought up another two-year contract—which Espo fought against on the grounds that if he had a big year the first season he'd be in an excellent bargaining position for a fat raise. But he lost his disagreement with Ivan, and settled for $17,500 and $20,000. He had a sixty-one point season in 1966–67, and acquired an unenviable reputation, advanced by his own boss Ivan, that he couldn't produce in the playoffs. Ivan shipped him to Boston in May 1967 along with Ken Hodge and Fred Stanfield in exchange for Gilles Marotte, Pit Martin, and Jack Norris, one of the dumbest trades ever for it sent three big strong forwards to the Bruins and turned them overnight from cellar-dwellers into contenders. The Bruins replaced the $20,000 portion of his two-year Hawk contract with a one-year pact for $22,500.

Upset that he'd been rejected by the high-flying Hawks and sent to a tail-ender, Phil determined to show the Bruins he didn't need Bobby Hull's stick to make him a big-leaguer. "I decided," he said, "to show the whole damned hockey world who Phil Esposito was."

And on that March weekend in 1969, of course, he was finally discovered when he scored his 100th point against Pittsburgh. The Boston papers began turning the spotlight on Esposito. So when the Stanley Cup playoffs rolled around, it was Esposito and not Bobby Orr who got all the attention at a pre-series press gathering in the Boston Garden.

This was held in a seedy relic called the Garden Club upstairs at the rink, a dreary retreat for Bruin directors, with framed racing prints hanging haphazard on the walls, a spotted gray rug of undistinguished weave, a stuffed sailfish suspended incongruously from the ceiling, and a couple of gazelle heads peering hopelessly from one wall—altogether an implausible amalgam of literary candle-power and dust-strewn wildlife. In this loose milieu, surrounded by the flower of Bostonian sporting prose, Esposito was the loose and colorful contrast, casual in conversation and in dress, with a black turtleneck under a bright yellow cardigan, black mod trousers and gleaming black boots. He was asked if he knew his name had brought a round of applause in the Canadian House of Commons for being the first player to score 100 points.

"Yeah, that'd be Terry Murphy did that," he grinned. "Terry's the member at the Soo, my home town. He lives about three cottages down the beach from us in the summer."

"Down the beach?" roared Johnny McKenzie, a Bruin rightwinger then, "What beach? What water?"

"Lake Superior," defended Esposito staunchly.

"Lake Superior?" echoed McKenzie. "The ice goes out for two days a year. Whattayuh do, go to your cottage for a weekend?"

"God, what a dingaling," said Esposito, regaining his composure and shaking his black head.

He was asked how he explained his year of 126 points. A hundred points, maybe, but 126?

"I feel like Midas, you know?" said Esposito, a big-boned, olive-complexioned man in a hair style surrounding his ears, with deep-set brown eyes, a gloomy cast to his features in repose, but quick to grin, a shambling guy of six-feet-one and 212 pounds. "The fact the club was offensive-minded helped. I mean, if we'd been stressing defense I'm not going to get half the shots, right. We scored 300 goals or so, you know, and one thing about it I'm going to get my share. Hell, the night I broke the record against New York I had thirteen shots. The way I figure it, I'll score on ten percent of my shots."

He was asked if the record was partly a reflection of the fact that in Boston he'd parked himself in front of the net, whereas in Chicago his job was to dig out the puck for Hull?

"Aw, that Chicago stuff was all out of proportion," he grunted. "Listen, I was a rookie then. I didn't have the experience or the confidence. One thing Bobby did for me, he gave me my philosophy about shooting. He used to say over and over, 'How you gonna put the puck in the net if you don't shoot the puck?' Look at Hull's record before he became an experienced hockey player. Compared to him I did pretty good."

He did, indeed. In Hull's first two seasons he scored thirteen and eighteen goals. In Espo's first two complete seasons he got his twenty-three and twenty-seven. Of course, Espo's leftwinger was Hull, drawing defenders away from Espoito.

"I give the guy all the credit in the world," he agreed readily. "Not just because I played with him but for another thing: In practices Billy Reay made me and Kenny Hodge skate with Hull. I mean, we'd do circuits of the rink following that man. You skate fifteen times around a rink with Hull setting your pace and you either become a skater or you drop."

Phil became a much better skater than most observers believe. Being big and gangling, he gives the deceptive impression of being slow, but against the Russians, for example, whose skates had wings, nobody pulled away from him. Another thing: It wasn't discovered until his third year in Chicago that Espo had mismatched feet, one was a size 11, the other a size 12. Until he got hockey boots to accommodate this disparity, he had chronic foot trouble. And at Boston he exploded the myth of playoff impotence; he popped goals from all angles.

When Espo was traded to the Bruins he immediately bought a home, positively establishing that he planned to be around for a spell. He and his wife Linda and their two daughters Laurie, born in 1964, and Carrie, four years later, settled in Salem, twenty miles north of Boston. In April 1973 he and Linda were legally separated.

In business away from the Boston Garden, he formed an alliance with a friend, Fred Sharf, who owned a sporting-goods business. They called it Phil Esposito Enterprises, endorsing a line of hockey equipment, seeking out manufacturers of top-quality merchandise made to Esposito's specifications. Within two years he had earned $20,000 in royalties from such gear bearing his name, and by 1973 the return had reached six figures on a gross of five million dollars.

For a man who didn't get people excited, he was doing very well indeed.

RED KELLY

[1927–   ]

O<small>N A COLD</small>, windswept January morning in 1959 Detroit
defenseman Red Kelly, a perennial all-star, was asked by his
employer, Jack Adams, if he'd mind going to Chicago where
the Red Wings had a date with the Black Hawks the following night. Ordinarily, it would be hard to fault the request:
Kelly had been among the thimbleful of top defensemen in
the NHL for a decade, chosen six times to the No. 1 All-Star
team and twice to No. 2. What made the request uncommon
this time was the fact that Kelly was wearing a plaster cast
over an ankle he'd broken only six *days* before.

Even so, Red said he'd give it a try. A doctor removed the
cast and taped the ankle from the instep almost to the knee.
Kelly played in Chicago the next night where, although he
could stand little pressure on his ankle and could put no
power into his stride, he helped the Wings to a 3–2 victory.
Moreover, he went on to finish out the NHL schedule without missing another game and wrapping up his twelfth season.

What made the incident memorable—indeed, it changed
Kelly's life—was not that he played with a serious injury—
hockey players as a group seem to have remarkable resis-

tance to pain—but that he never mentioned it as a reason for a dismal season. For strategic reasons the Detroit management kept his disability a secret, even when the Wings faltered and failed to make the playoffs for the first time in twenty-one years. Red did too, despite persistent public criticism of his decline. When one newspaperman submitted that Kelly's career was about ended, the player offered no rebuttal. Not until thirteen months later during an interview at Toronto's Royal York Hotel did he finally break silence. By then, the Red Wings were playing high in a new season and Red was back in form, but it had required nearly a year for him to get that way in long months of fretful rest and timorous exercise (he said later that his ankle hadn't begun to feel right until the new season was a month old). Finally, though, it became apparent that the requiem for a red-haired defenseman had been somewhat premature.

Yet, when Kelly did reveal the nature of the injury that had hobbled him, the story was picked up by Detroit papers and given banner treatment. Adams, the general manager, was livid. He hotly denied Kelly's account of his injury's nature and threatened to sue the writer. (By coincidence, the same writer was then working on a two-part magazine piece on the life of Adams in hockey, a ghosted autobiography; Adams wired the man in Toronto refusing to permit use of his name on the articles, though months later he relented.) Kelly was traded to the New York Rangers, but he refused to report. Adamant Adams refused to reconsider, and a week later traded Kelly to Toronto. This time, Red agreed to leave Detroit, largely because he had played junior hockey in Toronto and was familiar with the scene. There, he found a new life. Punch Imlach, the Leaf coach and general manager of the period, turned defensive all-star Kelly into a center. He finished out that season in his new position, and after seven more years in which Toronto won the Stanley Cup four times, Kelly finally concluded a twenty-year career as a player and became coach of the Los Angeles Kings of the NHL's new Western Division. They missed the division championship by a single point in Kelly's first season, and again made the playoffs in the second, finishing fourth. But Jack Kent Cooke, a restless man, dismissed Kelly after that second season, and Red moved on to Pittsburgh to coach the Penguins for most of four seasons, and then he rejoined his old team, the Maple Leafs, as coach.

During his two decades as a player Kelly compiled impressive credentials. Apart from his all-star record, he won the Lady Byng Trophy four times, was the first winner of the James Norris Trophy as the league's best defenseman, and played for eight Stanley Cup winners. During twenty seasons he was out of the playoffs only that one season when he played with a broken bone in his ankle, and his 164 playoff games were still a record as the NHL approached the mid-1970s, ten more than Gordie Howe, his one-time teammate.

But during that winter of 1959 when the Wings reeled, Kelly heard the anvil chorus. "Our trouble," said coach Sid Abel, as the team sank to the cellar and stayed there, "is that our veterans aren't producing. Our stars are letting us down." Whereupon he fined the players $100 each for lack of effort. And though no names were mentioned, Kelly was clearly a leading culprit. Of the other two Detroit bellwethers, Howe scored seventy-eight points that season and was fourth in the league's scoring tables, and goaltender Terry Sawchuk was named to the No. 2 All Star team. Clearly, then, neither of these was on the hook, leaving only Kelly of the starry veterans to carry the brunt of the coach's assessment. Around the league word was out that Red had joined the over-the-hill mob. But he didn't alibi, or even complain.

"The club announced that I had a sprain," he reflected during his Toronto hotel room interview, rubbing a hand over the area just below and in front of his main ankle bone. "I guess they didn't want other teams to know it was broken, and maybe start taking whacks at it. I didn't figure it was up to me to say anything, though I must admit now that I was surprised when I got fined the hundred."

He'd been pressed back into service on January 21 that season of 1958–59 after the Wings had dropped the first three of a four-game road trip. He was in Detroit, his leg in a cast, when Sawchuk was hurt in the third road game and unable to play at Chicago. Desperate Adams asked Kelly to help out, and brought in the veteran Bob Perreault from Hershey to play goal for Sawchuk. They won it, 3–2.

It wasn't the ankle pain alone that caused Kelly misery that night and in subsequent games, but also the taping.

"The ankle was tightly bound for games; and the tape was removed after them," he recalled. "Then my leg began to bleed every time the tape came off, so the doctor had to devise a smaller type of binding that just covered the ankle. But with it, I couldn't get leverage. If another player and I were shoving along the boards I always had to give way. I began taking more penalties than I usually do."

This was due to his loss of maneuverability. Beaten by an opposing forward, he was compelled to hook now and then, an unusual ploy for a Lady Byng winner. He took thirty-four minutes in penalties, modest by most standards but the second-highest of his long career and more than twice as many as he ever took in his subsequent seven-plus seasons for Toronto. The effect of the tender treatment he had to give the ankle was that Kelly became a stride or two slower in skating and a second or two slower in execution—the difference between being an ordinary performer and an extraordinary one. Then the rumors began eating at his confidence.

"I knew what was wrong, but I couldn't help getting discouraged," he reflected in the hotel-room confessional. "When you hear people say you're slipping you begin to wonder if they're right. That bothered me more than anything, I think—the nagging doubt. Ever since I was a kid I wanted to play hockey. The reason I never started smoking or drinking was that I figured I'd be able to play better and longer if I didn't. So I hated to think I was washed up."

Indirectly, a phone call restored Red's confidence. The call came late that June from the accomplished American figure skater, Andra McLaughlin. Two years earlier, in 1957, they had become engaged. Then the engagement was broken, and they didn't see each other or correspond for a year. Andra had been touring Africa, of all places, with an ice show, and when she landed in New York she phoned Kelly in Detroit.

"Red?" the voice said on the line.

"Yes."

"This is Andra."

"I know."

"Red, is it too late?"

"Naw, Andra, never."

Four days later they were married.

"Because of Andra I got my confidence back," Kelly reconstructed. "I've always been a little—ah—shy, but it's tough to be shy with Andra because she has such an outgoing personality. And having skated, she knows what it's like to be an athlete. She understands my moods, and she understood them then when I was having the trouble."

Red, christened Leonard Patrick, met Andra through Gordie Howe who had occasional dates years before with another championship skater, Barbara Ann Scott, the 1948 Olympic gold medal winner. Barbara Ann and Andra were touring with the Hollywood Ice Revue. When they reached Detroit Howe asked Red to go to dinner with them. Barbara Ann had to bow out at the last minute, but Andra was there.

"I was afraid to say much," Red recalled once, "but it didn't matter. Gordie did what talking there was, and I just looked at Andra."

After their marriage in Detroit on July 4, the Kellys spent part of July and all of August at hockey clinics in North Dakota, Saskatchewan, and Ontario where Red was an instructor. It was during these sessions that he discovered he liked teaching the game, and the seeds of his ambition to coach were sown. More important from a playing standpoint, the clinics gave him six weeks of ice time in which to strengthen the ankle. Then, in fall training, the Wings toured to the west coast playing exhibition games, and the ankle grew steadily stronger. Still, it bothered him occasionally until a month after the season opened.

Red always was a team man; although he earned his share of individual honors in his two decades as a big-leaguer they always came as secondary results of his contribution to the club. This was a point made by Punch Imlach about Red's term with the Leafs when, at thirty-three, he joined wholeheartedly in Imlach's decision to convert him into a center. Self-effacing, quiet, and contained, Kelly believed that to be successful a team had to work as a unit, forwards giving extra effort in their backchecking to help defensemen and then, in turn, even shouldering some of the goaltender's burden. For instance, when he played defense and was outnumbered by attackers on a break, his job wasn't to grab the puck-carrier or steer him to a corner but simply to try to delay the attackers by positioning himself to make them indecisive long enough for the forwards to get back and take a man.

"If the forward doesn't try his darnedest to get back, the defenseman after a while gets sick of trying," he expanded. "If the forward does charge like hang to get back, then it becomes a team effort, and pretty soon everybody's contributing a little extra."

Words like "hang" and "darn" were always as much a part of Kelly as his red hair and pale freckled features. He *never* swore. But he had his explosive moments. He once recalled a fight he'd had, a rare one, with Butch Bouchard, the one-time Canadian captain. "Big Butch clouted me across the top of my foot this night and I thought, 'Hey, he could have broken my foot.' I took a swing at him, a real hefty one because Butch was a huge man and I figured I'd only get the one swipe. I was really steaming, but I missed. Then he swung back and *he* missed, and then the linesmen broke us up. Some fight."

Another time, in a game at Toronto while he was still with the Red Wings, he swung his stick at Gerry Ehman of the Leafs, a most unusual act for Kelly, and he heatedly explained it later. "Hang it all, Ehman took a two-handed cut at my bad ankle. Doggone it, that's my livelihood. I respect the other guy's right to work; I expect him to respect mine. Surely everyone in the rink noticed, though, that I didn't come close to hitting him."

Kelly didn't get into more than half-a-dozen fights in his

128

two decades, but when he was a youngster growing up in Simcoe, Ontario, on the north shore of Lake Erie, things were different. "I fought a lot in Junior B, and in Midget before that," he said once. "I don't know, I guess I grew to have the notion that if I didn't fight I wasn't a hockey player. But when I got to St. Michael's College in Toronto and played for the St. Mike's Junior A's where Joe Primeau was the coach, I got a different slant. Meeting Joe was one of the lucky days of my life."

Primeau, a Hall of Fame member who centered Charlie Conacher and Busher Jackson on Toronto's unforgettable Kid Line, was one of hockey's most successful coaches, the only man ever to handle a Memorial Cup winner as national junior champion (Toronto St. Michael's), an Allan Cup winner as national senior champion (Toronto Marlboros), and a Stanley Cup winner (the Maple Leafs). He had a strong influence on Kelly's style and the shaping of Red's temperament.

Once, in Kelly's more rambunctious period, Primeau took him aside for a quiet talk. "How does it help this team," he asked the young redhead, "it you're sitting in the penalty box with a five-minute major? Maybe it helps your pride or your ego to put the slug on somebody, but it doesn't help us."

Primeau also gave Kelly more help in his practical development as a defenseman than anyone else. "He taught me how to play my position, how to skate backwards with a play, how to counter a developing play and even how to turn completely around without losing speed," Kelly remembered. Red made the Wings his first season out of St. Mike's and he always maintained that Primeau's instruction on the game's fundamentals permitted him to move into the big league from the juniors with enough steadiness, awareness, and play-making skill to stick.

"I was never told anything after I turned pro that I hadn't already been told by Joe," Red once said. "A lot of fellows are sent to the minors because they haven't learned positional play; they just don't know the fundamentals. Sure, it was a tougher league by far, and I made my mistakes, but each time they were pointed out, it was a case of being reminded of something Joe had told me."

For Maple Leaf fans, Kelly got to Toronto thirteen years late. St. Mike's was a junior affiliate of the Maple Leafs but Toronto missed out on him because he was a poor skater in his early years at the school. His father, Lawrence (Pete) Kelly, a farmer near Simcoe, raised the tuition for Red's education at St. Michael's from a none-too-bountiful purse. A family friend had assured the Kellys that he could arrange a trial for Red at the Maple Leaf tryout school at St. Catharines. When the arrangements collapsed Red was crestfallen, and Pete, aware of his son's absorption in hockey, sent him to St. Mike's where he waited on tables to help keep himself.

Red, the middle child in a family of two boys and three girls, didn't have much opportunity to develop his skating ability in the comparatively moderate temperatures of Simcoe, a town which then had no artificial rinks. He did more skating in the first of his four years at St. Mike's than he'd done in three years at Simcoe, and he developed quickly. The late Carson Cooper, who scouted him for Detroit, already had him earmarked for the Red Wings by the time Toronto realized he was a comer. Even so, the Leafs were hard to convince: one front-office genius bet Cooper a twenty-dollar hat that Red wouldn't survive ten games in his first NHL season, that he'd be shipped to the minors. Through twenty years, Red never knew a minor-league day. He didn't miss a game that first season. In fact, he only missed twelve games his first ten years despite twice breaking bones in his hands and accumulating the usual assortment of hemstitching. One of the more painful injuries in his Detroit career came during a Stanley Cup playoff against Toronto when Sid Smith of the Leafs backhanded a shot that caught him below the nose. The puck knocked out three teeth, opened a cut requiring eighteen stiches, and left his face so sore he couldn't close his mouth; he sipped eggnogs and gelatin for a week and lost twelve pounds while at the same time helping the Wings capture the Cup in the ensuing final playoff against the Canadiens.

With the Leafs Red never made either All Star team, but in Toronto that's par for the course; in Red's seven seasons, though the club kept splitting the winner's share of Stanley Cup payoffs, only Frank Mahovlich and Dave Keon were ever named among the All Star forwards. But they were team-play kind of teams Punch Imlach kept putting together, at least defensively, and Kelly fitted the pattern perfectly. Perhaps he would never have survived the switch from defense to forward with any other club, but with Toronto it wasn't unusual for Imlach to place four or five defensemen in his starting lineup, and hammer the hell out of the opposition early with tough, rugged body work. The Leafs from the days of King Clancy and the Kid Line were never a club reared or nurtured on offense. Over the years Toronto was almost as frequent a champion as Montreal, but the teams never had the color, verve, and panache of the Canadiens. Steady as she goes was always the Leaf watchword, grabbing and clutching, putting up a tough defense, battling and game, and eventually getting the goal that made it all worthwhile. A time-tested philosophy in any sport; the best defense always wins, even in a crazy-scoring game like basketball. The Superbowl is won in the trenches, the World Series on the mound. And in hockey, when the flamboyant Canadiens earned yet another Stanley Cup victory, it was the steady rocks in front of great goalers like Jacques Plante or Georges Vezina or Gump Worsley or Ken Dryden who have made the difference over the generations. Defense, defense, defense.

When Kelly went to Los Angeles, and later to Pittsburgh, as a coach, he took with him a solid fundamental knowledge, a quiet winning spirit, and a dedication to keeping the puck out of his own team's net as often as possible. But Red Kelly had one problem in both towns: when things got tough he could never look along the bench for a steadying hand and come up with a Red Kelly.

That was a terrible oversight.

HENRI RICHARD

[1936–   ]

$\mathcal{M}$AURICE RICHARD was a brooding, explosive saint in French Canada—but a saint, nonetheless—when his younger brother Henri began picking his way through adolescence toward what was to be a long, glittering life in the NHL. Adored as he was by the Forum legion of Montreal, the Rocket was mostly a burden to the boy who became the Pocket Rocket. Henri overcame long odds to become a star —physically, for he was a small man in a muscular game, and, more particularly, psychologically, because he lived for fifteen years in the shadow of his richly endowed brother.

When Henri was six years old his parents began taking him to the Forum to see his brother play for the worshipped Canadiens from two seats obtained for them by the twenty-one-year-old Maurice. Henri used to sit squeezed between his parents or on one of their laps to marvel at the flashing figures below. When Henri was seven his brother scored thirty-two goals to become an established star, and people sitting near the Richards in the Forum began pointing to Henri and saying that he was Maurice Richard's brother. And when Henri turned eight, his brother became the mighty Rocket Richard, an indomitable figure who scored fifty goals in fifty games, the first man ever to accomplish such a feat. So at school he was Rocket Richard's little brother.

Over the years, as the Rocket broke one scoring record after another, Henri was rarely allowed to forget that he was Maurice Richard's brother. Maurice was never *his* brother; he was always Maurice's brother. When he skated on *le ruisseau,* the stream, a nameless little brook that wound gently through the parish of Bordeaux on Montreal's northern outskirts where the eight Richard children were born, he was the Rocket's brother. When he played hockey on the outdoor rinks of Bordeaux for the Francois-de-Laval school, he was the Rocket's brother and the kids from rival teams in other parishes taunted him endlessly for it. When he played for the junior Canadiens, he was the Rocket's brother again, and some forgotten phrasemaker then labeled him the Pocket Rocket. He helped draw more than 12,000 people to Maple Leaf Gardens in Toronto one Sunday afternoon in 1954 for a meaningless junior game with the Toronto Marlboros, and the fans were generous in their applause, not for Henri Richard but for Rocket Richard's little brother, the Pocket. And in the NHL, after he'd made the grade, Henri was the target for jibes from the rival benches. As he'd skate by, he'd hear a high-pitched whine, "I'm gonna tell my brother on you!" Or, "Rocket, Rocket, I need you!" It went on and on and on.

There was also the physical burden. Except that Henri bore a certain facial resemblance to his brother—a long jawbone, an angular chin, and a small rather pinched mouth— they had little in common. They were teammates on the Canadiens for five seasons—from the autumn of 1955 when Henri broke in, until the autumn of 1960 when Maurice retired—and their dissimilarities were always apparent. The weight charts pinned to the wall of the Forum dressing room over a set of scales revealed that Maurice weighed 193 when a partially severed Achilles tendon sidelined him in November 1957. Henri's weight was 153½. Strapping Maurice, with sleek black hair and piercing coal-black eyes, stood five-feet-eleven. Henri, whose dark brown hair had a tendency to curl and whose eyes were a warm brown, showed four inches shorter on the charts at five-feet-seven. Just twenty then, Henri had a tough, compact body, along the lines of middleweight's, but he was still one of the smallest men in the league.

Nonetheless, Henri made it entirely on his own, and it wasn't until spring 1973 that he began seriously to talk of retirement. By then he was a veteran of thirty-seven with eighteen full seasons behind him, and he had even piled up *more* scoring points than the Rocket. On a night in early February when he scored his 966th point he moved one ahead of his brother on the all-time goals-and-assists list, though his 335 goals were a long way behind the Rocket's 544 and he'd required 1150 games to the Rocket's 978. Comparisons like these were inevitably made when Henri broke Maurice's mark but the little man brushed them aside. "I don't like this thing," he said one Sunday afternoon on NBC's television game of the week, by then his hair graying modishly along his ears. "He play the game twelve year ago. What I have done would not be compare, eh?"

But that, of course, was long after he'd proven he belonged. Perhaps the most graphic illustration of this was delivered in 1957 following the Achilles-tendon injury to brother Maurice when Henri was still something of a dubious big-leaguer. At the time of Rocket's injury he was leading the league in scoring, and Henri, who was centering a line on which Maurice was the rightwinger and Dickie Moore the leftwinger, was in second place. However, it was a questionable second place in some minds, a certain disposition around the league being to credit Henri's lofty position to the fact he was passing the puck to the game's greatest scorer. Obviously, every time the Rocket put the puck in the net, chances were good that Henri had picked up an assist.

But instead of skidding when Maurice was hurt, Henri continued to blossom on a makeshift line assembled by coach Toe Blake who switched Moore to the Rocket's rightwing spot and inserted Marcel Bonin at left wing. The seldom-used Bonin had had NHL experience at Boston and Detroit, but had spent the previous season in the minors with the Quebec Aces. Though the line should have lacked the cohesion of familiarity, young Richard continued to pile up points and by mid-season he and linemate Moore were engaged in a duel for the scoring lead. Indeed, when the season ended they were the league's top pair, Moore winning the championship with eighty-four points and Richard chasing him to the wire with eighty. Henri earned recognition at center on the No. 1 All Star team that season and, subsequently, he made the No. 2 team three times in the next decade, and by 1970 he had moved into heady atmosphere, the 300-goal club, a casement occupied by relatively few players.

As it turned out, however, the 1957–58 season was the brightest of Henri's many bright ones, and an illustration of the kind of performer he was came that year following an injury which forced him to the sidelines along with his brother. In back-to-back games with Toronto, Henri stayed home while the Canadiens played a scoreless tie at Maple Leaf Gardens and then insisted on playing the following night for the return engagement at the Forum.

He had an early chance at the Toronto net but was forced wide by a hooking defenseman. Instead of shooting from a bad angle, he held his precarious balance and took the puck on staggering steps toward the backboards, evaded a lunge from a Leaf trying to pin him, and manipulated the puck long enough for Marcel Bonin to dash toward the net. Henri's delicately timed quick flip to his hurtling wingman resulted in the first goal.

In the third period the Leafs came back to take a 3–2 lead with four minutes to play. Versatile Henri got the puck inside the Toronto blueline. When a forward zeroed in on him Henri whirled in a complete circle, cut past the forward and drew a defenseman to him. He stickhandled past *that* diving fellow and flipped the puck to the uncovered Bonin who popped it into the net. A minute later Henri eluded the defense again, set up Moore for the winning goal, and thereby concluded an evening in which he'd scored once and collected three assists.

Richard's attributes, apart from his dexterity, included a quick, hard wrist shot, a masterful flip from outside the blueline designed to bounce crazily ten to twenty feet from the net, and skating speed that his coach once called the swiftest he'd seen. "Faster than Morenz?" an incredulous listener asked Toe Blake. "Well," parried Blake, "I didn't see too much of Morenz. But from what I did see of him, yes, I'd have to say that young Richard is faster. Certainly there's not a player in the league today he can't pull away from—carrying the puck, too."

Perhaps Billy Reay, the wry coach of the Chicago Black Hawks, said it all.

"What do you think of Richard?" Reay was asked.

The coach allowed a slow smile.

"Which Richard?" he asked.

So after three seasons, the flashing form of the Pocket Rocket had proven it was in the NHL to stay, an elusive, crouching, mercurial figure wearing No. 16, difficult to hit because of his low-slung style, and one more of the endless number of swift dashing forms that seem almost a part of the Canadien heritage. Henri got among them the same way he bypassed the physical and psychological roadblock—with relentless persistence and determination.

A serious, quiet, gentlemanly fellow, Richard once said he couldn't remember a time when his ambition was to do anything but play for the Canadiens. He'd show an occasional turn towards homely humor, too. "If I do not play hoc*key*," he once said in his accented English, "den I have to work, eh?"

When he was six his brother Maurice bought him his first pair of skates and he went to *le ruisseau,* that little stream in Bordeaux, every day after school and every evening after supper where he skated, and skated, and skated. As he grew older and made the school team he played on the outdoor rinks of the quiet little parish after school and all day Saturday and Sunday. In the evenings when hockey gave way to general skating, he carried on without a stop from seven until the lights went out at 10:30. Usually he skated with a red-haired, brown-eyed girl named Lise Villiard. Henri's and Lise's older sisters were classmates who introduced the youngsters when Henri was ten.

"She didn't skate with any other fel*low,*" Henri smiled once, in recollection, "an' I didn' skate with any other girl." Henri and Lise were married in 1956 and bought a home in their native Bordeaux.

As a child Henri rarely saw his famous big brother except

138

on the ice. He was six when Maurice moved from the family home to marry black-haired Lucille Nochet. That left seven Richard children at home—four sons and three daughters, Henri being the second-youngest. They lived in a three-story, red-brick home on the edge of Bordeaux, which their father Onesime built in 1920. Onesime was a lean, reserved man who built freight cars in the Canadian Pacific Railway's shops at Angus, near Montreal, for nearly fifty years. Old friends such as Hector Dubois, the parish station master, once recalled that the fierce resolution for which Maurice became renowned and with which Henri made his way, was the heritage of Onesime.

"He is a determined worker of humble character," Dubois said at the time. "One year after he married Alice Laramee of the parish of St. Sacrement he built his own house in partnership with his father, and became its sole proprietor without any government help or subsidies. It was remarkable at that time."

Every morning after his sons became established hockey stars, Onesime caught a commuter train at Bordeaux to ride to the Angus shops, a small impassive man pacing the wooden platform in front of Bordeaux's dull-red frame station. One morning, the day after young Henri had returned to the Montreal lineup to help beat Toronto, Guy Huot, a family friend also waiting for the train, engaged Onesime in what Huot said was one of their typical exchanges over the years.

"*Que pensez-vous de la partie d'hier?*" asked Huot. (What do you think of the game last night?)

"Une bonne partie," said Richard *père* noncommittally.

"*Henri a fait plus que sa part,*" ventured Huot. (Henry did more than his part).

"*Il a bien joué,*" agreed Richard shortly. (He played well).

At this point, said Huot, the train arrived to end the conversation, or the train did not arrive and the conversation ended. Proud as he was of his boys, Onesime was not one to gloat.

During games at the Forum, Richard *père* was similarly a stoic. He would stare solemnly at the action and the only time he showed emotion was if one of his boys scored a goal. Then with a quick movement of his clenched right hand, like a fighter delivering a hook, he'd cry out, "Maurice!" or "Henri!" and return to his stolid vigilance.

Family friends recalled that all eight of the Richard children had this reserve together with Madame Richard, a handsome quiet woman built along comfortable lines. Toe Blake recalled a time when an American reporter, seeking an interview with Henri, asked Blake if the player spoke English.

Blake grinned. "I'm not sure that he even speaks French," the coach said. "He just doesn't speak."

Maurice and Henri rarely exchanged conversation in the Canadien dressing room, and when they did it was perfunctory. Maurice never gave Henri advice, and Henri was so constituted that he never could seek it from the Rocket. Guy Huot, the family friend in Bordeaux, once explained. "You know, those guy, they won't give—how you say?— *conseil?*" he asked.

"Counsel?"

"*Oui,* counsel—ah—instruction," he added emphatically. "Those guy in that fam*ily* never give it. And Henri does not want it. He is also relentless."

Henri never stinted in his praise for his brother—"No one will do as well as he has done," he said softly one time —yet theirs was not the usual brotherly relationship by a long shot. "When he left home I was so young," Henri tried to explain. "I'd hardly ever see him. He was like any other guy." It might have been significant that when Henri's parents took him to the Forum to watch the Canadiens he did not have eyes only for the Rocket. When he was asked what seemed a ridiculous question, "Who was your favorite player in those days?" his reply was surprising. "Ted Kennedy and Elmer Lach," he said quickly, naming center players for Toronto and the Canadiens. "And Red Kelly, too," he added. He was impressed with Kelly's determination, turning from an All-Star defenseman at Detroit to become a strong and solid center at Toronto.

Henri was asked why he'd picked Kennedy and Lach.

"They always get the faceoffs; they control the puck for the team. And they work like hell, too."

"What about Gordie Howe?"

"He seemed kind of lazy," said Henri. And then he added quickly, "But, of course, he is very good, you know dat."

"And what about Maurice?"

"Oh, Maurice," he said, savoring the name. "Nobody else can score a goal like him."

Henri, then, in striving to make the NHL, patterned himself after dogged players such as Kennedy and Lach, and such smooth effortless skaters as the relentless Kelly. And those faculties made up his game. He didn't have the Rocket's sudden explosive burst and even after five years in the league he was apprehensive when he learned his brother was going to retire.

"When he is gone, if I don't do so well, the people will remember him and for sure they're gonna say something," he once said with real concern, his soft brown eyes wistful.

Unwanted, the shadow of the Rocket was on young Henri

even when he'd visit the homes of his school friends. He recalled that when he was about eight a boy introduced him to
his father.

"So you're Rocket Richard's little brother."

"*Oui,*" said Henri shortly, and turned away.

When Henri was fourteen Maurice told Pete Morin,
coach of the junior Montreal Nationales, that he was going
to send his young brother around to see him. "He is to get
no favor," the Rocket said, scowling. "But if he is good I
want you to see him." When Henri showed up in the dressing room, a tiny fellow weighing about 105, Morin didn't
know him.

"Who are you?" he asked.

"Henri Richard."

"Are *you* the Rocket's brother?" blurted Morin.

"I am Henri Richard," bristled the youngster.

Someone unaware of Henri's fierce individuality once
asked him if he'd ever introduced himself to anyone as
Maurice Richard's brother.

Henri was appalled. "No, no," he said quickly. "I hate
dat."

He played against older and bigger players all through his
junior days with the Nationales and the Canadiens. Sam Pollock, the junior Canadiens coach who later became vice-president and general manager of the NHL club, once commented that he'd never seen Henri back away from trouble.
Whenever scraps developed, he was a terrier.

This was apparently an innate quality. From the dregs of
his memory Henri recalled that when he was ten a school
bully of fifteen blackened his eye in a scuffle. "Everybody
was afraid of dat guy," he related. "But I didn't want to run
away. I was afraid but I wasn't going to show him dat." Henri

stood his ground and took a beating.

Matt Pavelich, an NHL linesman for seventeen years, re-membered one fight Henri was involved in that he'll never forget—on New Year's Day 1958, Montreal at Boston.

"Henri hadn't been in the league very long and the play-ers were still giving it to him about being Rocket's brother. He was going along the boards and Fernie Flaman, a tough fireplug on the Boston defense, was rubbing him. Then Leo Labine leaped off the bench and took a swing at Henri. The players had been giving him a rough time all night.

"Well, Henri hauled off and hit Labine and split his eye-brow for eight stitches. That put Labine out. Then Jack Bionda came into it. Jack was a big son of a gun, about 210 pounds and six-foot-one or so, a real tough customer. Rich-ard hit him and split his nose. Twisted it across his face. That was him out. Fern Flaman came after Henri next. Fer-nie never lost too many. But he didn't handle Henri. It was a saw-off. I never would have believed it if I hadn't seen it. And yet Henri hasn't been in many fights since that one. The linesmen still talk about it."

Henri—when the English-speaking players on the Cana-diens say his name, it comes out Henry—Henri was still eli-gible for a year of junior hockey when he went to the Cana-diens training camp in the fall of 1955. He took his courage, or perhaps his doggedness, to the pro camp with him. He met his friend Guy Huot outside the Forum after a practice one day and Guy asked him if he thought he'd made the grade.

"Dey don' want me yet," Henri said grimly, "but I am going to make dem obliged to get me."

Toe Blake noted years later that he'd had no alternative but to sign Henri that year.

"When he was on the ice nobody else had the puck," Blake said. "No matter who I lined him up with, that line had the best scoring record in any given practice."

Maurice made no effort to influence management's decision on Henri. Once after a practice Dick Bacon, of the Montreal *Express,* asked Maurice how the kid was doing.

"He's ready now," the Rocket told Bacon.

"Did you tell anybody that?"

"No," Maurice said sharply. "It's up to the club to decide."

When the season opened the decision was to give Henri a three-game trial. An injury to Boom Boom Geoffrion gave Blake a chance to place Henri at rightwing beside Jean Beliveau and Bert Olmstead. He scored his first NHL goal against the New York Rangers on October 15. The Rocket scored twice in the same game, and the Canadiens won 4–1.

Blake moved Henri around from game to game after Geoffrion recovered, but resisted all impulse to team him with his brother. "I figured they might be jumpy together," Blake said. "Also, I thought Rock might pass up a lot of his own chances to feed Henri."

Then Chicago entered the Forum and the Canadiens ran into a couple of injuries and Blake was forced to team the brothers. They had never before played on a line, even in practice sessions, but in the third period Henri flipped a pass to Maurice, and Maurice resisted any impulse he might have had to return the puck to his *frère.* He blasted it into the Hawk net and, as Blake said later, "that was it." He teamed the Richards with Dickie Moore and the line stayed intact for two seasons. Blake once observed that the move might well have prolonged the Rocket's career.

"Henri put a lot of zip into the line, and the Rocket had

to skate faster than he had for years," Blake chuckled. "And oddly enough the move turned Rock into a better playmaker than he'd ever been, because, you know, he *did* like to give the puck to Henri. But he picked his spots, and he didn't make foolish passes when he was the man in the best position to fire."

At first Maurice had a low boiling point when Henri mixed with bigger players, and he'd storm to the rescue. But then once, with Maurice in the penalty box, Henri and Bill Gadsby, then a brash defenseman for the Rangers, began jolting in a corner, elbows and sticks going up.

"He came driving at me with that stick," Henri recalled. "I hit him and he fell to the ice. That was a break—if he'd hit me first I'd have been down, eh? The first punch matters, you know."

Anyway, Henri's performance was a revelation to his big brother in the penalty box. It taught him that Henri could look after Henri. "The first year I feel funny, worried like," Maurice related once. "I like to get hold of that fellow who hit Henri. But when I learn Henri can handle himself I start to hold back."

But on the ice or in the dressing room, he had few words for little Henri. If Henri scored he'd skate past him, mumble *"C'est bon, Henri,"* and let it go at that.

All question of the Rocket carrying the Pocket Rocket passed from most people's minds long before it escaped Henri's. Muzz Patrick, a New York vice-president, once provided graphic if indirect proof of Henri's complete acceptance in a conversation with Dink Carroll of the Montreal *Gazette.* This was along about Henri's third season with the Canadiens.

"I hear there's another Richard called Claude, playing for

the junior Canadiens," Patrick said. "What kind of a hockey player is he?"

It turned out that Claude didn't quite have the talent to stick in the NHL but, at the time, he was showing promise.

"How can you overlook him?" Carroll smiled at Patrick. "He's a Richard, isn't he?"

"My God," grunted Patrick in dismay. "Didn't Madame Richard have any daughters?"

TERRY SAWCHUK

[1929-1970]

Terry sawchuk, who died in a New York hospital on May 31, 1970, in his forty-first year, was regarded by numerous hockey authorities as the finest goaltender in NHL history, but surely no one ever endured a more star-crossed career. His life was an endless parade of aggravation and injury and even personal heartbreak. He endured everything that came his way until the May afternoon he failed to handle major intestinal surgery which followed a wrestling match with his New York Ranger teammate, Ron Stewart. When he died he was alone, divorced from the wife he married in 1953, separated from his children, and even held in high disfavor by most of the people he'd known through a twenty-year hockey history.

He was, literally, a physical and nervous wreck when the end came, all but washed up in the game he dominated from his goal position for two decades. He was through with the Rangers, just as he'd become expendable with the Los Angeles Kings before them, and the Toronto Maple Leafs, the Boston Bruins, and the Detroit Red Wings before *them*. Nonetheless, he'd been the best, even as recently as three years before he died when his unbelievably skilled play against Chicago and Montreal had helped produce an unexpected Stanley Cup for Toronto. That was, as he said himself, the peak of his great career, although he made his reputation when he was young and healthy, and as a member of the Red Wings had made the No. 1 All-Star team his rookie season, and in the two seasons following that. Amazingly, his average never topped 2.00 goals a game through his first five years at Detroit, a period in which he compiled fifty-six shutouts en route to a record 103, nine more than the runner-up, George Hainsworth, who made his mark with the Canadiens and the Leafs in the 1920s and 1930s. Sawchuk played in 971 regular-season games, sixty-five more than runner-up Glenn Hall.

Of all the stormy and troubled occupations, none is filled with more ups and downs than that of goaltender. The mere physical nature of the job compels its tenant to hurl himself, legs and arms asprawl, to a concrete-hard sheet of ice as many as thirty times in a sixty-minute game, then spring erect the next split second in the uncertain hope that a steel-hard rubber disc is not about to clunk him on the head at 120 miles an hour. Emotionally and psychologically, the big-league goaler faces even greater and more perilous shifts of fortune. His single mistake can cost his teammates the victory that represents thousands of dollars in playoff money, a charge that can never be made so strongly against the forward who misses an open net or the defenseman who misses a check. These mistakes can be amended; a goaltender's never can. He either stops the puck or the red light goes on.

And of all the masters of the craft, none suffered more ups and downs than Terry Sawchuk whose peregrinations over two decades were remarkably unpredictable even in so unpredictable a business. From the day he broke in it was always impossible to guess what could happen next to Saw-chuk, a moody man of exuberant peaks and mute depths whose name kept crowding into the headlines, for one rea-son or another, from the moment he turned professional in November of 1947 at the age of seventeen. Injuries, domestic crises, illness, accidents, numerous medical operations, illogi-cal trades, and the abnormal tensions of his pressure-cooker occupation plagued him constantly. His playing weight vac-illated from a high of 228 to a low of 146—a spread of eigh-ty-two pounds on a five-ten frame—and he totalled more than 400 facial stitches before adopting a mask in 1962, three of them on his right eyeball. He broke bones regularly, had concussions, arthritis, charley horses, mononucleosis. Surgery was necessary one time when he suffered a collapsed lung in a car accident. He was an unhappy man who in the late stages of his career was a morose loner given to periods of heavy drinking.

Almost any newsman who covered hockey in the latter Sawchuk years carried a Sawchuk story. His style was to lis-ten placidly to a question, then look the reporter in the eye, and snarl, "Get lost" or some euphemism thereof. A simple question, valid in his case, such as "How do you feel?" would elicit this response, "With my hands, dummy." Yet he once approached Jim Proudfoot, sports editor of the Toronto *Star,* to apologize for his surliness: "I get so wound up I don't know what I'm saying," he told Proudfoot. And as the writer said, "On balance, who couldn't forgive him for being irrita-ble; life was an ordeal for him."

Even hockey insiders were often surprised by the things that happened to Sawchuk. In 1955, pads deep in praise after he'd won his third Vezina Trophy in his first four years in the league and had helped the Wings earn the Stanley

Cup, Sawchuk was acquired by Boston to the undiluted astonishment of Boston's own general manager, Lynn Patrick.

"Oh, we'd been negotiating a trade with Detroit, all right," Patrick said, "but we'd been talking about several players, only one of them a goaltender. No goaler's name had been mentioned, however, and we thought we were talking about Glenn Hall, Edmonton's man in the Western league, who was owned by Detroit. In our wildest dreams we didn't think we could pry loose a guy of Sawchuk's status. When we found out that the mysterious goaltender of our negotiations was Terry, we were flabbergasted."

Detroit's general manager, the ostentatious Jack Adams, apparently decided that Hall, though only two years younger than Sawchuk, was a better long-range bet, a decision he was to rue when he and Hall stopped speaking for a season. Hall was eventually sold to Chicago.

Sawchuk, in turn, flabbergasted everybody halfway through his second season with Boston. Despite a virus blood ailment, mononucleosis, that hospitalized him for two weeks, he was so successful with the Bruins that he was named on the NHL's mid-season All-Star team. He greeted this news a few hours later by announcing he was through with hockey. In a hare-and-hounds act with pursuing reporters, he boarded a train for his home in Detroit. There, his physician announced, "Mr. Sawchuk is on the verge of a complete nervous breakdown."

Following *that,* Sawchuk turned up in goal for Detroit the following season, again to the surprise of Boston's Lynn Patrick.

"After they'd traded him, you know, I didn't think he'd want to go back there," Patrick said. "But Adams found out it was the only place he wanted to be, and we finally worked something out."

There were reports at the time that Sawchuk was simply homesick, but he scoffed at these. He lived with his wife and children in Union Lake, a suburb thirty-five miles from downtown Detroit, and the family stayed there while Terry was with the Bruins. "Sure, I missed them, but not that much," he said once. "Hell, I appreciated that hockey was my living and I told the Bruins when I was recovering from mono that I'd be back when I was better. Look, I left home in Winnipeg when I was a kid of fifteen. I've been on my own for a long time."

While Sawchuk insisted that moving back to his home had nothing to do with his recovery, doctors accustomed to the never-never land between physical and emotional disability weren't so sure. Sawchuk did have the symptoms of mono— enlargement of the lymph nodes in his neck, armpits, and groin—and a heavy feeling of fatigue.

"I lost twenty pounds in two weeks," he protested. "I was tired all the time and sometimes by the third period I wondered if I'd be able to finish the game." He was twenty-seven years old then. Once, driving home with his wife after Boston had played a game at the Detroit Olympia, he stopped his car for a sandwich and found he couldn't get out of it. "I just couldn't move my legs," he said later. "They felt like lead." On another trip home, "I'd just got inside the house when my legs gave out and I stumbled. I went into the den and broke down and cried. Pat tried to settle me down but I was scared. 'I'm through,' I told her. 'I don't know what's the matter with me and I'm through'."

But he rejoined the Bruins next morning. The club sent

him to a hospital for an examination. In two weeks, he was back in the cage. Then he decided he'd been released too soon.

"I was so weak the sisters were wheeling me to morning Mass in a wheelchair," he told a friend. "Then, for God's sake, early one morning I was told I could leave that day."

Lynn Patrick said he'd received a phone call that morning from Sawchuk telling him he felt fine. "So I figured he *was* fine and sent a car for him in the afternoon. He had a bad night in goal a while later and told me, 'You shouldn't have played me.' Not long after that, he left the club."

That was January 15, 1957. Remembering later, Sawchuk said he felt so depressed he decided to quit hockey. When he got to Detroit he stayed near home, first resting and relaxing, later playing golf at a municipal course operated by his father-in-law, Ed Morey. Soon he was playing twenty-seven holes a day.

"By midsummer I was feeling as well as I ever had in my life," he said later. "When I heard I'd been traded back to Detroit I won't deny I was glad to be playing at home again, but I still would have returned to the Bruins if they hadn't traded me."

The Sawchuks lived a quiet life at Union Lake in those days, the center of their existence being their television set during the season and Morey's golf course during the summer. Terry's wife, Pat, liked golf and played it when she could get away from her children. And when she and Terry could manage to slip off late in the evening they liked to spend an hour or so at her father's lounge, wearing informal clothes, sipping beer, and talking with the hockey fans who recognized the Red Wing goaltender. At those sessions Terry would talk earnestly and in an excited flow of words, shifting repeatedly in his chair. His wife said this was his style, except on game days.

"I never say a word to him on the day he's playing," she smiled once, remembering. "He's like an old bear. He blows up fast, but he gets over it just as fast. The kids used to bother him but, you know, Terry left home so early that he didn't know what homelife was like. It made him too independent."

Sawchuk used to concur with the last appraisal. "But that other thing, the way I am on the day of a game, well, hell, I *do* worry about every game. When our club goes good I worry it won't last; when we go bad I worry that maybe I'm the reason. I found I was worrying all day about the first period, when I'm sometimes cold, and then I'd figure when I got past it there were just two more periods to go, and then just one more. The crazy thing is, though, I don't worry at all while I'm on the ice, only when I'm sitting waiting. I always bend down as soon as I go into the net, and look at the goal posts. If they look close I know I'm gonna be okay, have a good night. But some nights those damn posts look a mile away."

In action, Sawchuk was one of the most acrobatic of all goaltenders. Someone once wrote that he didn't move so much as he exploded into a kind of desperate epileptic action; down the glove, up the arm, over the stick, up the leg pad—all in such incredibly swift succession that he resembled a human pinwheel. He played the whole game with a kind of pent-up tension, shouting at his teammates, crouching, straightening, diving, climbing up, his pale face drawn and tense before he covered it with a mask. His style likely accounted for the great number of facial cuts he accrued but the possibility he might be cut never occurred to him, and he had no fear. When he finally did take a mask, he said laconically of his face, "Why cut it up more?" Once, playing in Houston for Omaha, he got a stick in the eye and doctors feared he would lose it. He watched the operation through an arrangement of mirrors as the eyeball was laid on his cheek and three stitches were taken in it.

As a young man, he had a happy exuberance whenever things were going well. When he was seventeen and playing goal for the Windsor junior Spitfires across the river from Detroit, Jack Adams called him one day, gave him $2000 to sign a professional contract, and told him he was flying to Omaha that night to join the Red Wing farm club. Before leaving, Sawchuk sped to a Windsor bank where foreign exchange then favored American funds, and turned his money into about 2100 Canadian one-dollar bills. He carried the neatly packaged stacks to his room, closed the door, and hurled them against the wall, scattering the rug with a green cascade of bills. He wallowed around in them, grinning and chuckling, a chubby-faced adolescent who'd never before held a fraction as much money.

He weighed 175 when he departed for Omaha, and when he returned to his home in Winnipeg that spring his parents barely recognized him. He'd added thirty-five pounds. He figured 210 was his playing weight, and held that poundage for a time in the off-season, eating excessively, drinking beer and playing baseball for the Elmwood Giants in the Mandak League, composed of teams from Manitoba and North Dakota. He led the league in hitting .376 and got letters from the Pirates and the Cardinals to attend tryout schools, but he decided hockey was his game. Yet when he reported to the Wings that fall his weight had climbed to 228. Adams was horrified and ordered him onto a diet. When he got down to 200 he went off the diet but still continued to lose weight. By the time he'd become ill in Boston he was playing at 162, and had lost all idea of what his best playing weight should be. Perhaps the weight loss was traceable to his highly strung nervous system, or to the mental and physical problems that beset him. In 1957 he underwent an emotional upheaval when Pat sued him for divorce. When he heard of it, Jack Adams once said, "he broke down, cried, and sobbed." Then he went to Pat, talked about their difficulties, and was able to patch up the problems for several years, until divorce finally ended it. Soon after the reconciliation, though, he landed back in the hospital. He was driving home from the golf course when a tie-rod broke in the car's steering. The car crashed into a tree, with the steering wheel crushing Sawchuk's chest. In an ensuing operation his lung was collapsed to relieve the pressure.

Over the years he also had an emergency appendectomy and three operations on his right arm, which was two inches shorter than his left because of a boyhood football injury. During his first three NHL seasons, the arm—which he was never able to straighten after the accident—bothered him, and each summer he had chips removed. He estimated once that he'd had sixty chips taken out, twenty-two of which he kept, for inscrutable reasons, in a glass jar at home.

Things were never easy for him, even as a child, which perhaps partly explains why he was later able to take adversity in stride; he never knew anything else. His dad, Louis, was a tinsmith in Winnipeg when Terry was born at the beginning of the Depression. His brother Mike played goal at school so, as Terry used to say, "the pads were always around the house and I fell into them." Terry was ten when Mike died of a heart ailment at seventeen. Another brother,

Roger, died of pneumonia when he was a child. By fourteen Terry had worked at a foundry and for a sheet-metal company installing canopies over giant ovens in bakeries. He took his money home to his mother, who allowed him twenty-five cents a week.

While he was working, Sawchuk was usually able to find time for hockey. He was a boy of only twelve when Bob Kinnear, a Winnipeg scout for Detroit, got him onto a midget team sponsored by the Wings. As a fifteen-year-old he played junior (where the age limit was twenty) for the Winnipeg Rangers and was so promising that Detroit decided to transfer him to eastern Canada with the Wing-sponsored team at Galt, Ontario, in Junior A. He remembered once that he packed two pairs of pants and a red flannel jacket into a cardboard suitcase for the train trip to the east. His mother gave him a ten-dollar bill—"one of the few she ever had"—to buy essentials until he'd settled in Galt.

"There was a crap game in the smoker," he remembered. "After a long battle with my conscience I decided to get in. After an hour I'd won a hundred bucks, and I crouched there with the bills sweating in my hand, wanting to quit while I was ahead but being afraid to because I had most of the money. Finally, there was only one guy left who I hadn't cleaned out, and we rolled. He won it all."

He played a year at Galt, earning twenty dollars a week. "Well, actually, I got eight bucks a week," he was to recall. "The other twelve went to the landlady. I remember seeing a pair of shoes that I wanted desperately. They were twelve bucks. I faithfully gave the guy two dollars a week for six weeks, staring in the store window every day at the shoes that soon would be mine. Finally, I made the last payment, put on my new shoes, and walked proudly out of the store. I discovered walking down the street that I didn't like them any more, and never wore them again."

Altogether Sawchuk played twelve seasons for the Red Wings sandwiched around his two years with Boston. Prior to that he was rookie-of-the-year at Omaha, then Indianapolis in the American Hockey League and Detroit in the NHL, in consecutive seasons. At the summer meetings in June 1964, he was drafted by Toronto from the Red Wings and, sharing the goal job with another veteran, Johnny Bower, he got his name on the Vezina Trophy as the league's outstanding goaler. He stayed with the Leafs through three great seasons and then, with another Stanley Cup victory behind him, went to Los Angeles on a two-year contract for a salary reported at $80,000 in the expansion draft. He returned to Detroit for a kind of last hurrah, traded there after one mediocre season on the coast, got into eleven games with the Red Wings, then moved on to New York for what turned out to be his last year of hockey and of life. He played eight games for the Rangers, collecting his 103rd and final shutout among them, as Eddie Giacomin took on a back-breaking seventy starting assignments. Sawchuk played one Stanley Cup playoff game in the spring of 1970, a 5–3 loss to Boston, bringing his lifetime total to 101 playoff games, during which he collected an even dozen shutouts, third to Jacques Plante with fourteen and Turk Broda with thirteen. He was through with the Rangers then, for they were ready to bring Gilles Villemure to their cage permanently to share the load with Giacomin.

Through his last years Sawchuk remained injury prone, outlandish injuries. Somebody skated across his left hand, the one he caught pucks with, severing the tendons. He was hospitalized for an operation to remove a bowel obstruction, another to fuse bones in his spine, another to mend a mangled finger. The spinal surgery in 1966 disclosed two ruptured vertebrae, and repairs straightened a swayback condition and removed nagging minor disorders, such as headaches. Jim Proudfoot, the Toronto writer, once noted that Sawchuk had been unable to sleep for more than two hours at a stretch for years.

Then in May 1970 he went to a hospital for the last time. On the 31st of that month he died a day after emergency surgery to remove a collection of blood from his liver. He had been hospitalized a month following an operation for removal of an injured gall bladder. This after an incident involving his teammate Ron Stewart on April 29 in which they'd wrestled on the lawn of a house the two players shared at Long Beach, Long Island. They'd been arguing earlier in a tavern. District Attorney William Cahn said on June 8 after Sawchuk's death had been ruled accidental by a Nassau County grand jury that evidence indicated that at no time were any blows struck. "It was a verbal argument with lots of pushing and shoving," Cahn said. "It was an argument over a childish matter. It was a senseless death and completely accidental. The case is closed."

It was a sad and bizarre and lonely ending to a sad and bizarre and lonely life.

INDEX